*Dear Father Tom,*

# Can Catholics AND Evangelicals Agree about Purgatory AND THE Last Judgment?

*Enjoy!*

## BRETT SALKELD

*BN*

Paulist Press
New York/Mahwah, NJ

Cover and book design by Lynn Else

Library of Congress Cataloging-in-Publication Data

Salkeld, Brett.
    Can Catholics and evangelicals agree about purgatory and the last judgment? / Brett Salkeld.
        p. cm.
    Includes bibliographical references.
    ISBN 978-0-8091-4681-9 (alk. paper)
    1. Purgatory. 2. Catholic Church—Doctrines. 3. Evangelicalism. 4. Reformed Church—Doctrines. 5. Judgment Day. I. Title.
    BT843.S25 2011
    236′.5–dc22

                                              2010038011

Published by Paulist Press
997 Macarthur Boulevard
Mahwah, New Jersey 07430

www.paulistpress.com

Printed and bound in the
United States of America

# TABLE OF CONTENTS

To Sister Gill,
without whom this book could not have been written
and to Margaret,
without whom it could not have been published


Beloved, we are God's children now; what we will be
has not yet been revealed. What we do know is this:
when he is revealed, we will be like him, for we
will see him as he is.—*1 John 3:2*

# INTRODUCTION
## *"A Fond Thing, Vainly Invented"*

Since the division of Western Christianity in the six-teenth century, the doctrine of purgatory has been a point of contention between Catholic and Protestant Christians. Evangelical Protestants are at least as likely as their fellows to regard belief in purgatory as evidence of a faith that is not quite authentically Christian.[1] I pro-pose, however, that an investigation of the theological impetus for purgatory, the actual teaching of the Catholic Church concerning purgatory, and the corre-sponding teaching of the Evangelical community in its theology of judgment will indicate complementary insights about the fate of the "imperfect" Christian at death. Furthermore, I believe that the theologies of purgatory/judgment can offer a valuable insight on the nature of ecumenical dialogue itself.

In preparation for this project, I sent out a brief e-mail questionnaire to my Evangelical friends (who, in turn, passed it on to their Evangelical friends) just so that I could have some hard data to reflect on.[2] Almost without exception, the respondents pointed out one, or both, of the two principal concerns that Evangelicals have had with the doctrine of purgatory through the centuries: it is not directly evidenced in the Scriptures, and it detracts from the efficacy or necessity of Christ's sacrifice on the cross. Upon reflection such responses are not surprising. The student of the history of Christianity is well aware of the role played by purgatory in the genesis of the Reformation. It was, at least partly, in response to this doctrine (and its abuses) that the Reformers formulated the two pillars of their movement: *sola fide* and *sola scriptura*. To the Reformers and to their Evangelical descendants, purgatory violates both of these principles. It cannot, accordingly, be a tenet of authentic Christianity and is usually seen, as article twenty-two of the Anglican thirty-nine articles so poetically put it, as "a fond thing, vainly invented."[3]

Catholics, on the other hand, have continued to profess belief in purgatory. Such belief, it must be admitted, is often so corrupted by ill-informed popular piety as to leave it quite open to the charges that Evangelicals are wont to bring against it. Nevertheless, Catholics can point to a belief in some type of purification after death in the earliest centuries of the church and it is undisputed that Christians have always prayed for their dead.[4] Furthermore, they contend that purgatory properly understood is neither offensive to Scripture nor does it detract from the complete nature of the sacrifice Christ made on the cross. In purgatory, the Catholic sees the final pangs of the birth of God's new creation in Christ (John 16:19–22). [5]

At the Second Vatican Council, the Roman Catholic Church officially endorsed the modern ecumenical movement and encouraged its members to seek Christian unity through prayer and dialogue with their "separated brethren." Doctrines like purgatory that have historically divided Christians must become the subject of serious and open discussions for Jesus' prayer for the unity of the church to become a visible reality. In pursuing this dialogue, the church reminded the faithful of the "hierarchy of truths" in Catholic teaching.[6] That is to say, some doctrines are more central to an authentic Christian faith than others. The divinity of Christ must, for example, take precedence over, and inform, any teaching regarding the Virgin Mary. Purgatory is, admittedly, not a central Christian doctrine, but rather flows from and is subject to more central truths of the faith.

It is not, therefore, surprising that discussion of purgatory has not been high on the list of ecumenical priorities. Progress on several other fronts, such as the relation between Scripture and Tradition or the doctrine of justification, was a necessary prerequisite. A survey of the literature concerning purgatory since Vatican II is, nevertheless, disappointing. I was able to find only one ecumenically sensitive, book-length treatment of the topic (Robert Ombres' important *Theology of Purgatory*). Of the several quality articles written promoting an authentic doctrine of purgatory, a surprising number are written by non-Catholics[7] and, while this bodes well for ecumenical dialogue, it also indicates the degree to which Catholics have ignored this doctrine.[8] Indeed more sensitive work on this topic preceded the council than has followed it.[9] As pointed out in the preface to Ombres' work, it is not difficult, in "cleaning up" purgatory, to make it irrelevant.[10] Modern Catholics often hold the medieval view of purgatory or none at all.

The challenge, then, for an ecumenical treatment of purgatory from a Catholic perspective, is twofold. The first is to present the doctrine clearly and coherently with full awareness of the two major Evangelical concerns highlighted above. The second is to call on Catholics themselves to respond to this insight of their tradition in a way that reflects the broader truths that Catholics and Evangelicals profess together regarding the economy of salvation established by God the Father in Jesus Christ through the Holy Spirit.

Too often, Catholic practice confirms the criticisms leveled at the church regarding purgatory. If an open and ecumenically minded Evangelical were to pick up Father F. X. Shouppe's *Purgatory: Explained by the Lives and Legends of the Saints* in the hope of discovering what the Catholic Church really teaches about purgatory, that Evangelical could be forgiven for suggesting, even insisting, that purgatory is not an authentic

Christian doctrine. Here, for example, is a passage beginning on page 69:[11]

Father Mumford of the Company of Jesus, in his "Treatise on Charity towards the Departed," bases the long duration of Purgatory on a calculation of probability, which we shall give in substance. He goes out on the principle that, according to the words of the Holy Ghost, *The just man falls seven times a day* [Prov 24:16], that is to say, that even those who apply themselves most perfectly to the service of God, notwithstanding their good-will, commit a great number of faults in the infinitely pure eyes of God. We have but to enter into our conscience, and there analyse before God our thoughts, our words, and works, to be convinced of this sad effect of human misery. Oh! how easy it is to lack respect in prayer, to prefer our ease to the accomplishment of duty, to sin by vanity, by impatience, by sensuality, by uncharitable thoughts and words, by want of conformity to the will of God! The day is long; is it very difficult for even a virtuous person to commit, I do not say seven, but twenty or thirty of this kind of faults and imperfections?

Let us take a moderate estimate, and suppose that you commit about ten faults a day; at the end of 365 days you will have a sum of 3650 faults. Let us diminish, and, to facilitate the calculation, place it at 3000 per year. At the end of ten years this will amount to 30,000, and at the end of twenty years to 60,000. Suppose that of these 60,000 faults you have expiated one half by penance and good works, there will still remain 30,000 to be atoned for.

Let us continue our hypothesis: you die after these twenty years of virtuous life, and appear before God with a debt of 30,000 faults, which you must discharge in Purgatory. How much time will you need to accomplish this expiation? Suppose, on an average, each fault requires one hour of Purgatory. This measure is very moderate, if we judge by the revelations of the saints; but at any rate this will give you a Purgatory of 30,000 hours. Now, do you know how many years these 30,000 hours represent? Three years, three months and fifteen days. Thus a good Christian who watches over himself, who applies himself to penance and good works, finds himself liable to three years, three months and fifteen days of Purgatory.

The preceding calculation is based on an estimate which is lenient in the extreme. Now, if you extend the duration of pain, and, instead of an hour, you take a day for the expiation of a fault, if, instead of having nothing but venial sins, you bring before God a debt resulting

> from mortal sins, more or less numerous,
> which you formerly committed, if you assign,
> on the average, as St. Frances of Rome says,
> seven years for the expiation of one mortal sin,
> remitted as to the guilt, who does not see that
> we arrive at an appalling duration, and that the
> expiation may easily be prolonged for many
> years, and even for centuries?[12]

It is extremely difficult to salvage any sense of faith in the sacrifice of Christ from such a description. Such "crude accountancy…is a violation of the belief in God's forgiveness and a distortion of the basis of Christianity."[13] It makes Christian doctrine incomprehensible to the point that, as H. A. Reinhold put it, those who subscribe to it end up "in the small circle of sour looking and murderously strict puritans, while the rest of the world dances in the market-place to enjoy some relief before they descend into the fiery gloom prepared by a 'Savior' they cannot recognize."[14] If we are to measure eschatology by its reflection of the Christian virtue of hope,[15] this is bad eschatology.

The above does not represent—it must be insisted to both Evangelicals and Catholics—what the church understands herself to teach by affirming the doctrine of purgatory. Accordingly, the first step of this work must be to present what the church does, in fact, understand herself to teach regarding this doctrine. Without a clear view of this, any hope for progress in dialogue is unwarranted. For this reason, the first chapter will conclude with an attempt to provide an orthodox, ecumenically sensitive rationale for, and description of, purgatory as understood in the Catholic tradition. In the next chapter, it will be important to provide a brief sketch of the historical development of the doctrine, including its rejection at the time of the Reformation. The third section will endeavor to locate purgatory within the larger constellation of Christian beliefs to which it is secondary and which are less disputed between Catholics and Evangelicals. In the final section, a brief study of Evangelical theology regarding the last judgment will be undertaken in an attempt to demonstrate that many of the theological concerns that Catholics address by the doctrine of purgatory are addressed by Evangelicals in their judgment theology. Should this prove successful, the doctrine of purgatory need no longer be a stumbling block toward Christian unity. Indeed, it is the assertion and the hope of this book that a careful investigation of the theology of purgatory will indicate this currently divisive doctrine's value as an impetus for ecumenism.

# Review Questions

1.  How do you understand the relationship between
    purgatory and the Scriptures?

2.  How do you understand the relationship between
    purgatory and Christ's sacrifice on the cross?

3.  Which Christian doctrines do you see as being
    most closely related to the question of purgatory?
    Explain.

# Chapter 1
# WHY PURGATORY?

Two distinct but not unrelated issues are the bases for the emergence of the doctrine of purgatory. The first is the Christian practice of prayer for the dead. From the earliest records available it is clear that Christians have always prayed for their dead.[1] Western Christianity has understood this to imply purgatory.[2] This topic will be covered in more detail in the subsequent historical section. Here it should suffice to note that Western Christians, including Evangelicals and Catholics, see no point in praying for the dead in hell or in heaven. Those destinies are fixed and beyond hope, or need, of the aid of the Christian community. They draw, however, from this common conviction, opposite conclusions: Catholics affirm a state after death wherein prayer will be helpful (i.e., purgatory); Evangelicals, with most other heirs of the Reformation,[3] reject the practice of prayer for the dead.

The second impetus for the doctrine of purgatory is a rather pressing theological question, one felt by both Catholics and Evangelicals:[4] How do we account for the fact that "becoming a Christian" or "being saved" does not actually perfect anyone? Christianity contends that heaven is a perfect place, full of perfected people in perfect relationships. Furthermore, its founder, Jesus of Nazareth, has commissioned his followers to "be perfect, therefore, as your heavenly Father is perfect" (Matt 5:48). If we are to inhabit heaven and live up to Jesus' call, nothing less than perfection will do. In this light, the always candid Cardinal Ratzinger writes that "[s]imply to look at people with any degree of realism at all is to grasp the necessity of such a process [as purgatory]."[5] Purgatory can be understood as an affirmation of the biblical promise "that the one who began a good work among you will bring it to completion by the day of Jesus Christ" (Phil 1:6) even if we do not see this good work completed by the time of biological death.

Here it must be pointed out that the literature often suggests that purgatory emerged as Christians came to recognize some variant of the formula that "some people died who were, obviously, too good for eternal damnation and not good enough for heaven."[6] This is too simple. Evangelicals well know that, apart from the forgiveness offered in Jesus Christ, none of us are "good enough" for heaven. This formula leads too easily to a belief in works-righteousness that any ecumenical (or even theologically consistent) treatment of purgatory must strive to avoid. It is far more coherent to speak of Christians who are not yet fully sanctified, than to speak of people "not bad enough for hell or good enough for heaven."

It is unfortunately true that several centuries of confessional polemics[7] have contributed to widespread misinformation about the doctrine of purgatory. This is true for both Evangelicals and Catholics. While Evangelicals often do not fully understand what they reject when they deny purgatory, Catholics are frequently guilty of a "hardened antiProtestantism"[8] in their popular presentations of purgatory. Therefore, the first step in presenting the doctrine of purgatory is that of clearing up common misconceptions.[9]

# Clarifying Misconceptions

First of all, purgatory is not a second chance to accept the salvation offered in Jesus Christ. The orientation of one's soul is set at death as either accepting or rejecting God for eternity.[10] Like Evangelicals, Catholics affirm that heaven and hell are the only two final options for the human person.[11] Purgatory is not "a supposed middle state between heaven and hell,"[12] as proposed in one Protestant reference work.[13] Likewise, purgatory is not a temporary hell. In hell there is no hope. In purgatory one is assured of eternal salvation.[14] As such, purgatory must be distanced from any association with hell. It is, rather, the doorway to heaven. To use less spatial terms, purgatory can even be seen as the beginning of heaven, or one's first experience of heaven.

Historically, it is not accurate to suggest that purgatory was "invented" in the Middle Ages as a means of making money or of controlling the laity. Though it was undoubtedly used for both these purposes by unscrupulous individuals, even a brief investigation of the historical sources will demonstrate that purgatory's supposed "invention" is not an idea that can be sustained. Furthermore, there is evidence that, even in the preReformation church, such abuses of the doctrine were considered scandalous.[15]

Two more things must be noted, and they reflect the Evangelical concerns about Scripture and the efficacy of Christ's sacrifice on the cross. Catholic theologians do not claim that purgatory is directly evidenced in Scripture.[16] Attempts by Catholic apologists to point out proof texts that suggest that the Christian communities responsible for the production of the New Testament operated with a fully articulated doctrine of purgatory are rightly rejected by Evangelicals. Finally, and perhaps most important, purgatory is not a place where souls "work" for their salvation. With Evangelicals, Catholics affirm that salvation is wrought by the grace of God alone. With these prerequisites in mind, a brief examination of the basic features of purgatory, as understood by the Catholic Church, is now in order.[17]

According to traditional Catholic language, those who die in "mortal sin" go to hell. Those who die in a

14

"state of grace" go to heaven. Of those who die in a state of grace, it is supposed that some are perfected by the end of this earthly life and thus enter heaven directly, while others, with some remnant of sin still in them, require the "purification" of purgatory before attaining the beatific vision.[18] Roughly translated into Evangelical terms, this means that those who have rejected Christ are damned and those who have accepted him are saved, but of the saved, some are not yet ready to inhabit heaven at the time of biological death. Those who have chosen to follow Christ, but have not yet succeeded in letting his offer of sanctifying grace penetrate into every aspect of their lives, will have the opportunity to do so even after death.

It is important to note here that purgatory is, essentially, a continuation of the process of sanctification that each Christian undergoes in this life. The one important difference is that, death having sealed one's choice for God definitively, the possibility of rejecting God is not available to those in purgatory. With this caveat in mind, we can try to understand many aspects of purgatory by reflecting on the process of sanctification as experienced in this life[19] and, importantly, as reflected in the Scriptures.

It is appropriate here to make a brief foray into the vexed topic of "time," and its implications for this discussion. Sanctification obviously takes place in time during our earthly lives. How that is reflected postmortem is not an easy question. If Evangelicals consider the problem of incomplete sanctification, many will posit that its completion will happen at the moment of death so that entry into heaven is not "delayed."[20] It is a limitation of human language and comprehension that we must use temporal terms like "moment of death" to try to avoid temporality. Catholics affirm that anything that can be called a "process" requires something *like* time, but do not insist that such time would be experienced as time in this life is experienced. The two following comments should be helpful for orienting any discussion of time in an afterlife context. The first is from Cardinal Ratzinger, who notes that any "duration on the basis of temporal measurements derived from physics would be naïve and unproductive."[21] The second is from Robert Ombres, who posits that "'time' in purgatory can at the very least stand for the duration of the subject (soul) and its capacity for a multiplicity of acts."[22] In other words, while there is no use in discussing one's time in purgatory according to earth's calendars, some sort of time does seem philosophically necessary for change and, for most of us, perfection would constitute significant change.

Anglican theologian David Brown has written a very intriguing article that deals precisely with these questions.[23] In it, he challenges the idea of "instantaneous" perfection as essentially incomprehensible for temporal beings.[24] Perhaps his most interesting argument is that from "identity."[25] Imagine, he says, waking up tomorrow with your body and your memories, but with one important difference: you find yourself to be morally perfect. Temptations you found irresistible before are no longer comprehensible as temptations at all. Great struggles have been reduced to obvious choices. Personal relationships that once exasperated you are handled with the greatest ease and charity. Perhaps above all these others, "small" sins that you did not even recognize as such before are repugnant to you, and you cannot understand how you managed to justify them to yourself for so long. Brown asks, not unreasonably, whether this "new" person could legitimately be expected to identify itself with the one that went to bed the night before.[26] As Brian Horne points out, the Christian belief in the resurrection of the body insists that, "we shall, after death, be recognizably ourselves."[27] One might add that instantaneous, effortless perfection seems inconsistent with the picture of sanctification portrayed in the New Testament (see, for example, Paul's Letter to the Philippians) and experienced in the Christian life.

If Christians can accept that heaven requires perfection and that such perfection is only attained through a *process* of sanctification,[28] it remains to be shown how, precisely, Catholics understand purgatory as effecting such perfection. It cannot be the case that the hellish torments portrayed in popular piety work for the sanctification of the Christian soul. Rather, these seem to be arbitrary punishments of a vindictive deity. Evangelicals are right to insist that the punishment due for sin has been paid in full on our behalf. Not only do we not need to pay the penalty for sin, we are actually incapable of paying it.[29] Were we so capable, we would have no need of Christ's sacrifice. In this sense, traditional Catholic language concerning the "temporal punishment due for sin" is confusing.[30]

What needs to be understood is that Catholics understand sin, what we might call "sin proper," and the temporal effects of sin to be two different, if intrinsically linked, realities.[31] One accepting the forgiveness offered in Christ Jesus has their debt for "sin proper" cancelled, but the effects of sin are still readily apparent in the life of the believer and the world at large. This reflects the theological problem mentioned above: that Christians are not often seen to die in a state of perfection. Though their sins are forgiven, sins' effects are not yet completely erased. It is in this sense that St. Augustine wrote in his treatise *De Trinitate* that "it is one thing to remove a spear from the body, and another to heal the inflicted wound with treatment that follows."[32] The first step can be seen as (almost) "instantaneous." The second is a slow and gradual process. It is, nevertheless, difficult to overstate the importance of the first step. Removing the spear is a decisive and necessary prerequisite to any healing process. It is the effect sin has on the human person—which St. Augustine represents by the wound remaining after the spear is removed—that purgatory is concerned with, not "sin proper" that has been forgiven through Jesus Christ.

What is more, the healing of the effects of sin, though it is a slow and gradual process unlike what we might call "simple" forgiveness, is also effected by the grace of God through Christ. God having chosen not to perfect us immediately upon forgiving our sins does not mean we are left to our own devices.[33] In demanding perfection, God evidences his justice, but in helping us to slowly overcome what separates us from him, he evidences the respect he has for human freedom. By ensuring that whatever God "persuades [the human person] to do or accept arises from that individual's own moral self-understanding and perception,"[34] he affirms human dignity. God does not remove the sin in our lives by magically taking away our desire for it (see, for example, Rom 7:15). Rather he patiently teaches us, showing us our error and offering us the grace to overcome it. In this way we are involved enough in the process of sanctification at least to identify ourselves as the person sanctified. God's new creation is the redemption of the original. He has not scrapped the whole project and started again.

# Examples of Purification

The Catholic tradition has recognized two aspects of sin that remain after what has been called "simple" forgiveness and that call for purgatory. This can best be illustrated by way of example. In her introduction to Dante's *Purgatory*, Dorothy Sayers provides a nuanced but succinct exposition of the logic that some sort of purification is required even after justification in Christ.[35] I have loosely paraphrased her work as follows in the interest of brevity but recommend the original as far more comprehensive:

Imagine that, in anger, you break your friend's vase but, after reflection, recognize your fault, apologize, and are granted forgiveness. This is roughly equivalent to the justification offered by Christ. Your relationship with your friend (and God) is restored. Two things remain, however: the vase is still broken, and the fault in yourself that led you to break it in the first place has not been addressed. In order for justice to be complete, the vase must be repaired or replaced, and you must amend yourself so that such an incident will not happen again. If you were indeed truly sorry, you would desire both things. This is what is meant by the term "satisfaction." Someone dying without replacing the vase or amending themselves, that is, not having made satisfaction, would not, however, face condemnation. Through Christ our relationship with God has been restored. The person is saved. The problem is that we are showing up in heaven with a broken vase or, more to the point, our broken selves. Knowing that "what is destined for God must be perfect"[36] and that those in relationship with God are not condemned, we must posit some process by which we are perfected.

This process must in some way take account of both the internal and external aspects of sin outlined above.[37] In the above example, the vase exemplifies the fact that, when we sin, we do damage to more than just ourselves. Bigham writes pointedly that a murder creates both a victim and a murderer.[38] The Catholic Church has at times been guilty of obscuring the meaning of the doctrine of purgatory by emphasizing the external demands of justice. That is to say, it has sometimes focused more on fixing the vase than on fixing the person. Language about sanctifying the sinner sounds humane and Christian. Language concerned with punishment for broken vases sounds juridical and risks ignoring the reality of God's offer of forgiveness. The overemphasis on the juridical aspect of purgatory has given "the whole doctrine of purgatory a bad reputation from which it has not recovered in Protestant thought."[39]

Any contemporary account of the doctrine of purgatory must certainly present the internal "amendment of character"[40] as the primary rationale for acknowledging a purgative process. It is in the perfection of the human person that the "deeper meaning"[41] of the doctrine lies. It is not enough, however, simply to deemphasize the juridical, external aspect of purgatory. We must reimagine it. Otherwise, it risks being a skeleton in the Catholic closet, something we quietly maintain while we avoid discussing it with our (more squeamish) dialogue partners. There is, of course, the temptation to drop this aspect altogether but, if the Catholic tradition has accepted the logic outlined above, that would mean denying the reality of our sins' effects on the world around us. This seems outside the realm of possibility.

One promising possibility for reimagining the "external" aspect of purgatory has been put forward by Cardinal Ratzinger. Sachs explains:

> Ratzinger suggests those in purgatory are still related to history by the enduring effect of their actions on others. The guilt and suffering which go on in the world because of me are a part of me and therefore affect me. Purgatory means suffering through what I have left behind on earth.[42]

This suggestion accounts for the reality of the effects one's sins have on the world but also manages to maintain the primacy of the perfection of the human person in purgatory. One is not arbitrarily punished for particular sins, but one sees those sins in their full reality, something nearly impossible in this life. Indeed, it is hard to imagine repenting fully of something that one does not understand fully. Surely it is the case in this life that the degree of our repentance is dependent on the degree to which we recognize our wrongdoing. Who has not, in their journey toward God, been called to greater repentance and greater dependence on the mercy of God by being shown the depth of their sin?

Purgatory completes this process by allowing us to see the fullness of our sin in the light of God's love.

It has been maintained, nevertheless, that the more important aspect of purgatory is what has been called the "internal," and that the external only makes sense in relation to the perfection of the human person so that that person can inhabit heaven. It is to this element that we must now turn our attention. The following example is designed specifically to demonstrate the internal effects that sin has on the human person.

John has an addiction to pornography. In the course of dealing with this addiction he has come to recognize that his faith community does not forbid the use of pornography because it is fun and exciting, but because it actually prevents him from being the person he wants to be and having the relationships with others that he would like to have. He has noticed that he stares inappropriately at women in public places and is embarrassed when they too notice it. He has found it difficult to respect his girlfriend's wishes regarding their physical intimacy because he has less self-control than he expects from himself. Sometimes he even chooses to stay home to indulge his habit rather than spending time with friends or accomplishing some productive work.

John is eventually convinced of his need for repentance. He seeks God's forgiveness and asks for help in his community of faith. His sins are forgiven and he is reconciled to God. He is subsequently, with the help of

God's grace and the support of the Christian community, successful in avoiding pornography. Still, John notices that he continues to stare at women and he cannot always control himself when he is intimate with his girlfriend. He also has to work hard to reengage the friendships he had neglected and to make productive use of his time.

By asking for, and receiving, the forgiveness offered by God, John has had Augustine's spear removed from his life—but he is still wounded. He can see at least some of the effects of this "wounded-ness" in his everyday life. It is clear to him that he still needs to be perfected. The state to which Christians are called and whose achievement is, in fact, promised, is clearly not made manifest by what has been called simple forgiveness.

Now, it is entirely possible that, through God's grace, John will be healed of these remnants of his sin in this life, but it is easy to imagine reasons why he might not be: lack of recognition of the gravity of his condition, negligence, or, perhaps most obviously, untimely death. There is, in the Catholic tradition, a recognition that death may work to bring about a fuller realization of one's state before God and thus bring about deeper repentance, perhaps repentance so complete that nothing remains for purgatory. This seems to be the case for the good thief. With death imminent he was granted the grace of literally a face-to-face meeting with God. At the other extreme we can imagine John, still slave to some old habits, taking a second look at the girl in the short skirt as he steps absentmindedly into the currently unavailable crosswalk.

Having genuinely repented and having had his relationship with God restored, the remnant of sin in John's soul cannot cost him his salvation. Only a rejection of God's forgiveness can do that. He is, nevertheless, not prepared for heaven. A heaven full of people with bad moral habits, people ready to use, manipulate, and control one another, people who have not yet allowed the fullness of the redemption offered in Christ into every aspect of their lives would not really be heaven at all—it would just be more earth.

## Purification as an Encounter

This brings us to the essence of the doctrine of purgatory. How is John, or how are any of us, to be purified so as to be able to inhabit heaven? The Catholic tradition has suggested various metaphors, but they are all summed up in one essential reality: we are purified by an encounter with Jesus Christ—the divine judge and the living God. The burning holiness of God will be unmistakable before the repentant sinner. Too often in the tradition the image of fire has been used as an instrument of torture, but there is a better use for it. The Scriptures use fire to describe God's purifying love for us (Mal 3:2). Joseph Pieper points out the aptitude of the metaphor of fire for God's love because, like fire,

God's love "consumes everything and transforms everything into itself."[43] To inhabit heaven we must be conformed to Christ. One of the most beautiful and sublime accounts of purgatory available in the Catholic tradition was written by St. Catherine of Genoa. She too makes use of the biblical metaphor of the refiner's fire to describe the state of the soul in purgatory:

> The soul is like gold, which, the more it is fired, the more it becomes pure and the more its imperfections are obliterated. Fire works this same way on all material things. The soul, however, cannot be annihilated in God, but is purified more and more in itself, so that, dying to itself it rests purely in God. Gold, when it is purified to 24 carats, will no longer be consumed by the fire toward which it is drawn, because the fire cannot consume anything that is not imperfection. In the same way, the divine fire works on the soul....[A]fter the soul is purified to 24 carats, it is rendered immutable because there remains nothing left that can be consumed. The soul, having been purified in this way and being held, still, in the fire, feels no longer any pain. On the contrary it remains in the fire of the divine love for all eternity, containing in itself nothing contrary to that love. [The author's translation from the Italian is intended to express Catherine's thought than

to be precisely literal. See the note for the original text being cited].[44]

The beauty of this metaphor is that it captures the essence of purgatory without the need to posit a "third place," away from God. The soul is changed by the encounter with God's love. This love, though painful when first encountered by the less-than-fully-sanctified person, is the environment in which we will operate for eternity. As Catherine notes, gold that has been purified to 24 carats no longer "suffers" in the furnace.

Here it is necessary to address the question of suffering in purgatory. Though the tradition does not insist on material fire and literal "pain of the sense,"[45] it has repeatedly affirmed that the process of purgatory will be painful, even intensely so. We cannot understand this pain as inflicted from outside by God in some sort of retributive sense. There is no theological justification for a loving God to punish sin arbitrarily. (Catholics and Evangelicals both need to be careful of this regarding any theology of the crucifixion.) Rather, "the punishment of sin is ultimately the intrinsic suffering caused by sin itself, not an additional act of retribution by God."[46] It is when this is forgotten, and the pains of purgatory are understood as God's retribution against sinful people, that popular piety becomes "absolutely unintelligible, nay almost unorthodox [because it] fits so poorly into the dogmas of redemption and salvation."[47]

God does not inflict pain on those in purgatory; the pain derives "from the fact that my own guilt will stand in unbearable contrast to the absolute love which God has for me."[48] Again, we can recognize the truth of this statement by reflecting on our experience of love in this life. Who would not be pained to see unconditional love still alive in one whom they have hurt? A wife taking back an adulterous husband. An abused child forgiving the abusive parent. We are at once grateful, and made more fully aware of our unworthiness by such acts of love. The encounter with God after death must be profoundly more moving, for we will see with greater clarity the depth of our betrayal and the infinity of the love God has for us.

Despite the intensity of the pain, we must remember that pain is not the essence of purgatory, only the means by which it must be accomplished. Brown contends that "no sense can be given to any moral development that is bereft of [pain], since being pained at the discovery of the wrong one has done would seem integral to any properly moral recognition that it was in fact harm-doing."[49] C. S. Lewis has written that the treatment given in purgatory "will be the one required, whether it hurts little or much."[50] Bigham says in a memorable phrase that "in purgatory, punishment does more than fit the crime; it fits the criminal."[51]

The tradition further insists that, rather than fearing these pains, the souls in purgatory will embrace them. St. Catherine says the joy of the suffering souls in purgatory is exceeded only by the joy of the purified souls in heaven.[52] Fully aware that they are drawn closer and closer to the love of God as the remnants of their sinful lives are stripped away, those in purgatory rejoice even as they suffer. We can only hint at this joy by identifying the way we not only tolerate, but genuinely enjoy, activities like a painful therapeutic massage or acupuncture because we recognize in them the means for our recovery. Likewise, the souls in purgatory will rejoice at knowing the whole truth about themselves, even when that truth hurts immensely, because it must be acknowledged in order to be redeemed.

One further aspect of the Catholic doctrine of purgatory remains to be discussed before this section can be considered complete. As previously noted, one of the bases for the development of the doctrine was the Christian conviction that prayer could be offered for the dead. This aspect of Catholic piety is often perceived as quasi-pagan. Certainly, if purgatory is rejected, the need for it is difficult to discern. If purgatory is accepted, however, the practice acquires some Christian meaning. We must briefly investigate this meaning now.

First, it is essential to note that the overarching doctrine under which this practice can be understood is the Christian belief in the Communion of Saints. This will be dealt with in more detail later, but for now we can appeal to the pithy statement of Ombres, who notes that "the ultimate criterion is not biological but Christological—am I with Christ."[53] The Body of

Christ—the Communion of Saints—is not circum-
scribed by death. St. Thomas Aquinas captured the
mind of the church well when he taught that "caritas,
quae est vinculum uniens membra Ecclesiae, non
solum ad vivos se extendit, sed etiam ad mortuos qui in
caritate decedunt; caritas enim vita corporis non fini-
tur"[54] ("love, which is the bond uniting the members of
the Church, does not extend only to the living, but also
to the dead who have departed in love; for love is not
limited by the life of the body" [author's translation]).

However, an important theological problem
becomes apparent here. How exactly does prayer for the
dead help them to bear more easily the burden of purgatory? J. P. Arendzen outlines the problem well: "The
Holy Souls could not enter the sight of God before they
were inwardly, essentially and intrinsically prepared
for it....if God should for some external reason, for
someone else's sake, admit them unprepared in his presence, they would beg to return to purgatory, for heaven
would not be heaven to them."[55] Arendzen notes the
beginning of the solution to this problem when he says
that if "the faithful can help them with their prayers,
they can only do so from within, not from without."[56]
Beyond this, however, he seems to offer only that we
are here in the face of a "great mystery."[57]

As true as this might be, I propose that we can shed
a little more light on the problem. Aquinas understood
that it was the bonds of love in Christ, who conquered
death, that make communion among the saints possi-

ble even across the boundary of death. In light of this, can we not understand prayers and offerings for the dead as acts of love? Surely we know from experience in this life that the single most effective way to teach someone about God's love is to love them with it. Every time we act out of genuine charity, we bring both ourselves and others a little closer to God. Given the grace by God to know that those on earth still love them—remember that those in purgatory are fully aware of how much hurt they have caused their loved ones in earthly life—would not this love impel them to a greater understanding of God's love and forgiveness? Would not knowing that a bitter quarrel has been abandoned in favor of prayers for one's soul move one to forgiveness and charity as well? Again, when we reflect on what we know about the love of God from this life, where we see but "through a glass, darkly," we can better appreciate how that love can operate when we meet it face-to-face.

## Review Questions

1.  Discuss the two basic reasons for the development of the doctrine of purgatory. Might you suggest any other factors?

2.  Which misconceptions about purgatory does the author note? Have you encountered any of these? Where? Would you add anything to the list?

3. Have you ever experienced the difference between what the author calls sin proper and the effects of sin? Where have you recognized the damage done by sin even after forgiveness is granted and accepted? Might forgiveness change these effects of sin in any way? How?

4. How do you understand the internal and external aspects of satisfaction? How do they relate to sanctification?

5. What role does an encounter with Christ play in your understanding of purgatory? How does a Christological reading of this doctrine make it more coherent? How does it relate to the idea of suffering in purgatory?

6. What does it mean that prayer for the dead must work from within, not from without? How does the author propose understanding the function of prayer in the sanctification of the dead? How else might we understand prayer for the dead?

# Chapter 2
# HISTORICAL
# CONSIDERATIONS

When one turns to the literature regarding the historical development of the doctrine of purgatory, the initial impression is that two irreconcilable positions are being promoted. Some authors, mostly Catholic, find evidence for purgatory in the earliest writings of the church fathers. Others, largely Protestant, suggest that nothing like purgatory emerges until at least the sixth century, and then only on dubious grounds. Furthermore, almost all agree that the noun form *purgatorium* does not emerge until the mid-twelfth century, but while some see this as the "birth" of purgatory, others insist that it is only one small step in the development of the doctrine.[1]

This problem is illuminated when one recognizes that the two groups of authors are using the word *purgatory* to mean two quite different realities. The former, largely Catholic group, who find purgatory as far back as the *Didache*,[2] is seeking any indication of a

Christian belief in some postmortem period of purification. The latter group, following Luther,[3] considers
no one to affirm purgatory whose ideas do not bear
some resemblance to purgatory as conceived in the
medieval penitential system.

This situation is, actually, encouraging in the
sphere of ecumenical dialogue. It provides correctives
for the errors of both groups. Catholics need to look outside of the medieval penitential system for their images
and explanations of purgatory. As the Congregation for
the Doctrine of the Faith warns, "the danger of imaginative and arbitrary representations is particularly to
be feared because their excess forms a great part of the
difficulties which Christian faith often encounters."[4]
Evangelicals often need to recognize that the content of
the Catholic faith concerning the doctrine of purgatory
is in many ways quite different from the purgatory
rejected at the Reformation. Furthermore, both these
groups of authors seem to agree, at least implicitly, with
a central premise of this book—namely that, for reasons both historical and theological, only a doctrine of
purgatory that is far removed from the penitential system of the High Middle Ages can be the subject of ecumenical dialogue. Indeed, officially and doctrinally,
Catholics affirm simply "the existence of purifying
pains in the afterlife, and the value of prayers for the
relief of suffering souls."[5]

The remainder of this chapter will focus on a brief
elucidation of the development of the doctrine of pur-

gatory with an awareness of the two aforementioned definitions one finds in the literature. It is to be hoped that such an ecumenically sensitive presentation will be able to find resources in the history of the doctrine that can lead Catholics and Evangelicals to greater unity on this issue.

# Scriptural Perspectives

Any study of the development of Christian doctrine must begin with Scripture. As noted in chapter 1, Evangelicals are correct to reject any arguments by Catholic apologists that seem to suggest that some passages in the New Testament indicate a fully formed doctrine in the early Christian communities that could rightly be called purgatory.[6] Nevertheless, it is important to note a few passages of Scripture, as they are important in the historical development of the doctrine. The first is 2 Maccabees 12:38–46. This work is, from the Evangelical perspective, apocryphal. It cannot be overlooked, however, as the fathers of the church regarded it as Scripture[7] and often referred to it in their reflections on the value of prayer for members of the Christian community who had died. Because Catholics and Evangelicals do not share a common evaluation of the canonicity of this work, we must not make too many claims on it. It should suffice here to point out that, whether or not it is the inspired Word of God, it is, presumably, an accurate representation of Jewish piety in the period leading up to the incarnation. As such, Jesus and the early Christian community would have been aware of the practice of praying for the dead as it was practiced in the Jewish community. There is no historical evidence that Christians abandoned this practice, and ample evidence that they continued it.

The second important passage is found in the first Letter of Paul to the Corinthians, chapter 3:12–15:

> Now if anyone builds on the foundation with gold, silver, precious stones, wood, hay, straw—the work of each builder will become visible, for the Day will disclose it, because it will be revealed with fire, and the fire will test what sort of work each has done. If what has been built on the foundation survives, the builder will receive a reward. If the work is burned, the builder will suffer loss; the builder will be saved, but only as through fire.

More than any other passage, this one has been understood to imply a doctrine of purgatory. It is easy to understand how someone with an existing framework that includes purgatory would see the doctrine here. It must be admitted, however, that without such a framework no one would necessarily be persuaded into a doctrine of purgatory by it. For this project, it is important to note that, though the passage cannot be claimed to represent purgatory, reflection on this passage contributed to the development of the doctrine. It is not evidence of, but a foundation for, purgatory. As such its insights must be compatible with any conclusions this book may reach.

These two passages are, without doubt, the most important in the history of the development of the doctrine.[8] We can note here three more passages that have occasionally entered the discussion on purgatory and the logic by which they were included. Two come from the Gospel of Matthew. In the first, Jesus teaches that sin against the Holy Spirit will not be forgiven in this age or the next (Matt 12:32), implying the possibility of forgiveness in some subsequent age. In the second, Jesus tells a parable in which the king punishes a slave by handing him over "to be tortured until he should pay his entire debt" (Matt 18:34), implying that the torture will not be eternal. Lastly, the Book of Revelation is invoked to demonstrate the necessity of purity for entering into heaven (Rev 21:27). While postmortem forgiveness, temporary punishment, and the purity of heaven are all important for the doctrine of purgatory, commentators agree that none of these passages are, neither singularly nor together, sufficient grounds on which to posit the doctrine.

# Patristic Understanding

In the patristic period we encounter the first explicit Christian teaching regarding the possibility of

a postmortem experience in which the elect are purified. Many passages from the fathers demonstrate the
emergence of this belief among Christians, often with
reference to prayer for the dead.[9] They cannot all be
investigated here. Instead, select passages of historical
or doctrinal significance will be noted. Of particular
interest are the *Dialogues* of Gregory the Great in
which Luther discerns the first hints of the medieval
doctrine of purgatory. Our study of the patristic era
will conclude with an investigation of that document.

Graham Keith notes the fluidity of eschatology in
the early church,[10] and it is wise not to evaluate the
orthodoxy of each statement of the early church by our
current understanding. It is more important to see the
way in which seminal figures in the Christian tradition
have grappled with the theological issues that purgatory addresses, and follow how these reflections gradually became more systematized until they resembled
what the Catholic Church today understands by the
term "purgatory."

Aaron Milavec has suggested that the first hint of
purgatory in the patristic literature is to be found in
the *Didache*. This is roughly a century before anything
else emerges in the literature that suggests purgatory.[11]
Milavec's contention is based on his reading of *Didache*
16.5, which speaks of a "burning process of testing"
and teaches that those "having remained firm in their
faith will be saved by the curse itself."[12] Milavec's argument rests on his identification of "the burning process

of testing" as "the curse" while traditional exegesis has understood the curse as being a veiled reference to Christ.[13] If Milavec's proposal is found to have merit, the *Didache* is certainly the earliest instance of purgatorial ideas in the patristic literature.

More widely accepted as the earliest writing to speak of postmortem purification by fire is St. Clement of Alexandria's *Stromata*. In it we read of those who die reconciled to God but without having completed penance on earth being "sanctified [by] a fire which is not a consuming fire like the fire of a forge, but an intelligent fire which penetrates the soul and is traversed by it."[14] Here Clement distinguishes between fire that destroys and fire that purifies,[15] a distinction that will become essential for future theologizing about purgatory. Further, he has given us a historical clue as to the situation in the church that led to speculation about postmortem purification. In early Christianity, postbaptismal sin was a grave concern requiring severe penance before ties with the community could be reestablished. It was not believed, however, that someone who died after seeking forgiveness but before completing the requisite penance would be damned. Still, something remained imperfect in that person's relationship with the Body of Christ. The possibility of postmortem purification addressed this problem.[16] That fire would be the metaphor for this purification is entirely understandable from the biblical tradition as exemplified by the passage from 1 Corinthians mentioned above.[17]

St. Gregory of Nyssa's (335–394) teaching is worthy of mention for two reasons: first, the striking resemblance of his work to modern theologies of purgatory and second, his status as a representative of Eastern Christianity, especially because we know that most of the reflection that led to the current understanding of theology took place in the West. In *De Anima et Resurrectione* he writes:

> For [God], the one goal is this, the perfection of the universe through each man individually, the fulfillment of our nature. Some of us are purged of evil in this life, some are cured of it through fire in the after-life....The different degrees of virtue and vice in our life will be revealed in our participating more quickly or more slowly in the blessedness we hope for....The healing of the soul will be purification from evil and this cannot be accomplished without suffering.[18]

Note that this looks significantly like modern purgatory; it is not yet colored with medieval notions of punishment or satisfaction for particular sins. The key here is the character of the individual. Healing the individual is the purpose, and suffering is necessary only in as much as it attends the treatment.[19]

An entire study could be devoted to the doctrine of purgatory in the works of St. Augustine.[20] Here it must suffice to examine his insistence on prayer for the dead and its implications for his belief in a process of post-mortem purification.[21] For Augustine there were three categories of people at death: the condemned, the blessed, and the blessed but unprepared, which correspond to the threefold possibility of hell, heaven, and purgatory.[22] In *City of God* he writes:

> On behalf of certain of the dead the prayer of the Church or of pious individuals is heard, but only on behalf of those who are regenerate in Christ and whose life in the body was neither so bad that they should be judged unworthy of such a mercy nor yet so good that they be found not to need it.[23]

This is not, it must be insisted, works-righteousness. Before any mention of the moral qualities of the individual, Augustine makes it clear that we are speaking here of those "regenerate in Christ." For Augustine, prayer for the dead implied that they were not beyond the aid of the church and that some, at least, had need of it. This logic has been preserved in the Western church to this day, whether by the acceptance of purgatory or by the rejection of prayers for the dead.

When Keith, a Protestant scholar who opposes the idea of purgatory, notes that Augustine's ideas were eventually "elaborated into a full-scale doctrine of Purgatory," which "Augustine would have deplored,"[24] he carefully spells out the medieval juridical framework of purgatory. This reflects the dynamic noted at the beginning of this chapter. Keith's concern is salutary, even though his work was not written with an eye to ecumenical considerations. Indeed, what Le Goff perceives as doubts in Augustine concerning "the timing, the subjects, the concreteness, or the location of *post mortem* purgation"[25] could be perceived rather as orthodoxy. At a time when Catholicism must distance itself from a juridical and quasi geographical image of purgatory, it is very useful that a figure as influential as Augustine declined to define such variables. As such, Augustine is the last major figure belonging solely to the patristic period. In the *Dialogues* of St. Gregory the Great we can perceive the end of the patristic era and the beginning of the medieval conception of purgatory.

## Medieval Developments

In Book IV of the *Dialogues*, we have the first examples of stories of souls beyond the grave experiencing pain and suffering that is subsequently relieved by the prayers of the faithful, particularly the offering of the Mass. It is this development that is recognized as the first hint of purgatory for those whose definition requires purgatory to reflect the penitential system of the Middle Ages.[26] What is identified as purgatory, and

what is correspondingly rejected, is the state of tor-
ment described in Gregory's *exempla* from which souls
find relief only after some offering, particularly the
Mass, on their behalf. This quasi-geographical state
from which sinners are released upon the completion
of certain "works" is difficult to reconcile with salvation being a pure gift of God's grace. Here emerges,
moreover, the understanding of the doctrine that
would later be abused for economic gain. Gregory's age
was one of "avid supernaturalism"[27] and the subtle,
restrained reflections on postmortem purification that
we find in the earlier fathers were now abandoned in
favor of a highly imaginative portrayal of life after
death. Because of the authority of Gregory, *Dialogues*
"became the model for anecdotes"[28] about purgatory
throughout the Middle Ages. Under its influence "the
concept of a possible state or condition of purification
after death became that of a place with the material element of fire as a means of purification."[29] This imaginative construction was an essential element in the
development of the purgatory rejected by the Reformers
in the sixteenth century.

Interestingly, in 1987, Francis Clark published *The
Pseudo-Gregorian Dialogues*.[30] As the title indicates,
Clark contends that the *Dialogues* were not produced
by Gregory at all. This would have come as a relief to
Martin Luther, who had complained of Gregory's
inconsistencies[31] and M. Gatch, who writes that "[t]he
passages of Dialogues IV which have been regarded as

43

teaching a doctrine of purgatory are...riddled with problems of interpretation."[32] Even the council fathers at Trent, who considered Gregory's *Dialogues* authoritative because of the eminence of their author,[33] may have been happy at this development that, if true, removes some of "those things which tend to a certain kind of curiousity or superstition, or which savour of filthy lucre,"[34] from the corpus of Gregory's work.

Though it is not the task of this book to assess Clark's and, after him, McEniery's claims definitively, it is certainly worth noting that addressing the problem of Gregory's imaginative representations of purgatory, and their subsequent effect on medieval piety, becomes much easier for the Catholic tradition if Gregory is not, in fact, the author. Indeed, another of Gregory's works, *Moralia*, seems much more coherent with both ancient and modern conceptions of purgatory.[35] As McEniery suggests, "[a]s embodied in the Dialogues, the doctrine of purgatory is an offence to many outside the Roman Communion and may well be a case...where...the stumbling block of faith has been established in quite the wrong place."[36]

The juridical formulation of purgatory that began with Gregory became highly systematized in the subsequent centuries. It is beyond the scope of this presentation to trace all the connections between indulgences, suffrages, mortal and venial sin, private Masses, and the abuses that attended them. It should suffice to say that purgatory, as it is commonly understood by Evangelicals, and by still too many Catholics, emerged in this period. It is significant that in 997, Odilo, abbot of Cluny, introduced the Feast of All Souls to counter concern that the rich may have more access to aid while in purgatory due to their ability to endow churches or monasteries with funds to procure Masses for their souls.[37] The noun form *purgatorium* made its first appearance in the mid-twelfth century[38] and within one hundred years, Thomas Aquinas could teach that "to deny Purgatory is to speak against divine justice and to resist the authority of the Church."[39] Thomas's own theology is commendable for avoiding the excesses of the medieval penitential system. This is important for ecumenical dialogue because of the towering stature of Aquinas in Catholic theology.

It was easy, within the medieval penitential system, to regard salvation as achieved mechanically, not through faith, or even through a life of virtue, but rather through a series of prescribed acts that took on an almost magical quality. God could be understood as being manipulated into forgiveness through the appropriate use of the church's sacramental system. Relationship with God and dependence on God's grace were easily overlooked. In this system, purgatory was portrayed as punishment by which sin was expiated with the effect that Christ's sacrifice could easily lose its singular importance in the minds of the faithful. Within this milieu Aquinas wrote that, in purgatory, guilt was not remitted "per poenam, sed per usum gratiae, quae est effectus divinae misericordiae"[40] ("through punishment, but through the use of grace, which is the effect of divine mercy"[author's translation]). Furthermore, he upheld the subjective, internal character of the punishment of purgatory when the popular conception made the punishments of God external, arbitrary, and even vindictive. To say that "acerbitas illius poenae non est tantum ex quantitate peccati, quantum ex dispositione puniti"[41] ("the severity of that punishment is not so much according to the degree of the sin, but according to the disposition of the one being punished" [author's translation]) leaves open an idea of purgatory that does not impugn the character of God or deny the efficacy of the crucifixion and resurrection.

Modern ecumenists can be thankful that the greatest theologian of the age set forth a doctrine of purgatory that is compatible with the critiques that have since dismantled the medieval conception. They also owe a debt of gratitude to the Greek delegations at the Council of Lyon[42] and especially the Council of Ferrara-Florence. It was at these councils that the excesses of the medieval system could most easily have entered the realm of official teaching. We have, however, been spared the effort of integrating many of those excesses into our dialogue due to the restraint the Greeks demanded in the definition they affirmed regarding postmortem purification.

While the doctrine had been increasingly systematized in the Western church, the Greeks had maintained merely the constant Christian practice of prayer for the dead and the affirmation of the early church that those prayers could help those who died and who might be suffering some sort of purification. The Greeks had no language of "satisfaction" being made for sin,[43] and particularly abhorred the idea of material fire, doubting whether it could be applied to disembodied souls.[44]

Due to their collective lack of reflection on the topic prior to the debates at Ferrara-Florence, the Greeks initially found it difficult to respond to the highly systematized doctrine of the Latins, but their thought was gradually articulated, and they held firm to their convictions so that the final teaching of the council on purgatory, signed by both parties, said simply "Also, if truly penitent people die in the love of God before they have made satisfaction for acts and omissions by worthy fruits of repentance, their souls are cleansed after death by cleansing pains; and the suffrages of the living faithful avail them in giving relief from such pains, that is, sacrifices of masses [a footnote here says "Latin sacrifices of masses, Greek holy sacrifices"], prayers, almsgiving and other acts of devotion which have been customarily performed by some of the faithful for others of the faithful in accordance with the church's ordinances."[45] The lack of any geographical language and, especially, the absence of material fire as a means of purification are particularly noteworthy.

It is useful here to indicate the remarkable treatise

of St. Catherine of Genoa.[46] Just a couple of decades before the scandal of indulgence sales precipitated the events in Germany that would fracture Western Christianity, she composed what became, essentially, the last work written on purgatory that did not operate in a milieu of interdenominational polemic. As such, this work cannot be recommended too highly. Moreover, her basic vision is so undefiled by the perversions that had crept into the doctrine (and precipitated the practices that scandalized the Reformers in the first place) that Anglican Edmund Pusey has suggested that, if hers had been the widespread teaching on purgatory, the Anglicans need not have condemned the doctrine at all in their thirty-nine articles.[47]

Catherine's was not, however, the widespread teaching on purgatory. We can already see signs, even before Luther, that the abuse of the doctrine, and particularly its connection with indulgences, was becoming suspect. Catherine herself warned her readers against putting false hope in a plenary indulgence and thereby cheapening God's grace.[48] Larissa Taylor found that French preachers at the time (1460–1560) seldom preached about purgatory and suggests that they may have avoided the topic so as not to be associated with the indulgence vendors.[49] In 1518, the University of Paris heard such vendors described as "false, ridiculous, scandalous and dangerous preachers who extort from the poor"[50] by the king's confessor.

Such a situation was, of course, instrumental in the

assault on the conscience of one German Augustinian monk. Indeed, Martin Luther was so scandalized by such behavior that he was compelled to take the stand that would eventually lead to the division of Western Christendom. As indicated in the introduction, the Reformers saw the rejection of purgatory as a necessary corollary of the two pillars of their movement, *sola fide* and *sola scriptura*. But just as new understandings of the role of faith and of Scripture shaped the view of purgatory, the rejection of purgatory necessarily impacted other areas of Christian theology. The interconnectedness of this doctrine with other articles of faith can be overwhelming.[51] When something as integral to the medieval Christian worldview as purgatory is discarded, compensation must be made. The issues it addresses must be addressed in other theological contexts. Looking at how the issues addressed by purgatory are dealt with in other Christian traditions is essential for ecumenical dialogue on the subject. This theme will be investigated in chapter 4 in the realm of eschatology and the Evangelical theology of judgment.[52]

# The Council of Trent

In the face of criticism from the Reformers, the Catholic Church firmly maintained the teaching on purgatory at the Council of Trent, though quarter was given to the fact that the doctrine had been misrepre-

sented and abused. The Decree on Purgatory from
Trent (1563) states:

> The Catholic Church, instructed by the Holy
> Spirit and in accordance with sacred Scripture
> and the ancient Tradition of the Fathers, has
> taught in the holy Councils and most recently
> in this ecumenical Council that there is a pur-
> gatory and that the souls detained there are
> helped by the acts of intercession of the faith-
> ful, and especially by the acceptable sacrifice of
> the altar.
>
> Therefore this holy Council commands the
> bishops to strive diligently that the sound doc-
> trine of purgatory, handed down by the Holy
> Fathers and the sacred Councils, be believed by
> the faithful and that it be adhered to, taught
> and preached everywhere.
>
> But let the more difficult and subtle ques-
> tions which do not make for edification and,
> for the most part, are not conducive to an
> increase of piety (cf. I Tim 1:4), be excluded
> from the popular sermons to uneducated
> people. Likewise they should not permit opin-
> ions that are doubtful and tainted with error to
> be spread and exposed. As for those things that
> belong to the realm of curiosity or superstition,
> or smack of dishonorable gain, they should for-

bid them as scandalous and injurious to the faithful.[53]

Like the Council of Ferrara-Florence, Trent, in the first paragraph of its statement, insists only that purgatory exists and that souls therein can be aided by the prayers of the faithful. As previously mentioned, these are the only features of a Catholic theology of purgatory that actually have the character of "official teaching."[54] The third paragraph is, in fact, an acknowledgment of at least some of the Reformers' concerns regarding purgatory.

Catholic theology regarding purgatory has been largely static since Trent.[55] McGuire notes the relationship of purgatory to the growth of eucharistic devotion since Trent and suggests that this relationship was strengthened by an emphasis on the Communion of Saints during this time.[56] While official theology at Trent was "restrained, modest and prudent,"[57] the language of "penal satisfaction" and "expiation" that had come to dominate in the Middle Ages maintained its prominence in popular Catholic understandings of purgatory until at least Vatican II. When, in light of the council, that language became understood as obscuring the central truths of Christianity, purgatory was largely dropped from Catholic observance except in traditionalist circles that maintain the old usages and piety. Modern Catholicism, while maintaining purgatory, has done little to reimagine it.

Significantly, Vatican II mentions purgatory in *Lumen Gentium*, the Dogmatic Constitution on the Church. It is thus placed in the context of the Communion of Saints, as any patristic notion of postmortem purification would have been, rather than dealt with, as at Trent, in relation to justification.[58] This shift is important. At Trent, the council fathers were reacting to a particular claim regarding justification and consequently felt the need to deal with purgatory in relation to that central question. The new, and ancient, context of the Communion of Saints means that we are less likely to see presentations of purgatory that refer to our "expiating" our sins and more likely to see presentations concerned with our conformation to Christ and his Body.

In the twentieth century, purgatory is often briefly mentioned in the works that theologians devote to eschatology (e.g., Ratzinger, Hellwig, Hayes, von Balthasar, Rahner), but it is rarely treated in a comprehensive matter. These modern theologians, writing both before and after Vatican II, rarely speak of "penal satisfaction." The focus of the last century was certainly on the transformative, cleansing nature of purgatory. Avery Dulles notes that the late "John Paul II, in texts familiar to me, makes no mention of punishment or expiation in purgatory."[59] John Paul's successor, Joseph Ratzinger, similarly avoided such an understanding of purgatory in his work *Eschatology: Death and Eternal Life*.[60]

Though the Catholic faithful often subscribe to a vision of purgatory that is either scandalous or content-less, the resources are available in modern Catholic theology to address this issue. It is the nature of ecumenical dialogue that the resources to address difficulties within one's own communion are the same resources necessary to dialogue with Christians of other traditions.

# Review Questions

1. Why do Catholics and Protestants find the beginnings of the doctrine of purgatory at such different points in the development of Christianity?

2. What does it mean to say that a passage in Scripture is not evidence of a belief in purgatory, but rather foundational for the development of that belief? What other Christian doctrines are you familiar with that were articulated only slowly as the implications of Scripture were reflected on in the community?

3. How is ecumenism helped by the thought of Thomas Aquinas and Catherine of Genoa concerning purgatory? What importance is there in the fact that Catholics before Luther were also scandalized by the abuse of the doctrine?

# Chapter 3
# THE THEOLOGICAL CONTEXT OF PURGATORY

At this juncture it should be sufficiently clear that neither Catholics nor Evangelicals believe that the doctrine of purgatory is explicitly taught in the Scriptures. Interestingly, this same claim can be made about the doctrine of the Trinity. Both groups wholeheartedly affirm this doctrine, but its presence in Scripture is, at best, cloudy. Rather than an articulation of the Trinity, the Scriptures present us with claims about the nature of the divine that are quite difficult to reconcile. Jesus says, "The Father and I are one" in John 10:30, but in Matthew 24:36 he teaches that "about that day and hour no one knows, neither the angels of heaven, nor the Son, but only the Father." The early Christian community did not immediately affirm the Trinity as we understand it. Instead, they were forced to try to reconcile seemingly diverse claims about Jesus, his divinity, and his relationship to the Father and the Holy Spirit.

In the same way, the doctrine of purgatory is not taught in the Scriptures because it was not articulated by the early Christian communities that produced them. Rather, later reflection on truths taught in Scripture led the Christian community to systematize its thought into what became the doctrine of purgatory. Robert Ombres writes that in studying purgatory from a scriptural perspective, "we have to reconstruct the trajectories and parameters, the drift, that would generate and require subsequent theologizing."[1] The reader is by now familiar with the basic outlines of this process historically and with what is and is not essential to the doctrine of purgatory. With this in mind, we must now turn to an investigation of several biblical teachings that relate to purgatory.

This section will examine the teachings of Scripture regarding heaven and hell, the Communion of Saints, the value of suffering, the presence of God, and the goal of Christian perfection. This investigation obviously cannot be comprehensive. Instead, it will try to expound what Catholics and Evangelicals hold in common regarding these issues in the hope of placing purgatory within its broader scriptural and ecclesiological contexts.

One methodological note is in order. One of the difficulties of ecumenical dialogue is the fact that no theologian, publication, official statement, or other such recognized body can speak authoritatively on behalf of the Evangelical community. As such this chapter will limit itself to the teaching of several Evangelical theological dictionaries. It is understood that not every Evangelical will subscribe to the teachings therein, but it is hoped that, in their preparation, these dictionaries have striven to present a basic consensus of Evangelicals on a given topic. As a Catholic, the author hopes that, in pursuing such a course, he will be able to avoid misrepresenting the views of the Evangelical community even as he recognizes the likelihood that individuals in that community will dispute particular insights.

# Heaven and Hell

Both Catholics and Evangelicals affirm that the Bible teaches only two final possibilities that exist as the final destiny of the human person: heaven and hell.[2] Father Ron Rolheiser writes that "we're either at God's right hand or at God's left hand, sheep or goats. There's no third option."[3] The human person is meant for God. In heaven the human person will be fulfilled, but in hell the human person will be lost forever. At the most basic level, heaven consists of life with God in eternity, and hell is the deprivation of that life.[4]

The Old Testament demonstrates an increasing awareness of life after death among the Israelite community.[5] From the very earliest times, however, the Israelites affirmed that to be with Yahweh is the fullness of life, and to be without him is the worst possible outcome.[6] Though the full implications of this unfolded only gradually—as the Israelites came to recognize Yahweh as Lord not just of Israel, but of the whole world, and not just of biological life, but of eternity— the fundamental affirmation that to be with God is the ultimate good of the human person underlies all scriptural teaching on eschatology.

In the New Testament, the most obvious expression of this may be in John 14:3, where Jesus tells his followers, "if I go and prepare a place for you, I will come again and will take you to myself, so that where I am, there you may be also." It is also present in the teaching of Paul in, for example, Philippians 1:23[7] and 1 Thessalonians 4:17.[8]

Christianity has understood this final union with Christ as one possibility for human persons. As such, the *possibility* of not being with Christ is seen as logically necessary. Catholic Zachary Hayes writes:

> If the positive outcome of life is a union of love with God, such union presupposes freedom. But freedom in turn involves the possibility of refusing the gift of God's self-communication. Therefore, the very conditions for the possibility of the Christian view of positive fulfillment are simultaneously the reasons why theology holds that hell is a possibility.[9]

Entries in Evangelical dictionaries also affirm hell as the possibility of life without Christ; for example:

That [the] exclusion from God's presence is the
real significance of hell is clear in Jesus' teaching (Mt. 7:23; 10:32f.) and in Paul, who does
not mention Gehenna but whose images of
"destruction", "death" and "corruption" refer to
separation from God, the source of all true life.[10]

Another adds "the wicked in hell are excluded from
God's loving presence and the 'life' for which humans
were originally created (John 5:29)."[11]

Both Catholics and Evangelicals have, in their
respective traditions, representations of hell as positive
punishment from God (sometimes portrayed as God's
retributive wrath for sin), and as the intrinsic result of
a life of sin that rejected God's forgiveness. These two
visions are often held in tension,[12] partly due to the
imagery used in the Bible to describe hell. This tension
is also evident in the Catholic tradition concerning
purgatory. While God's retributive wrath may be
invoked in our description of hell because of the wit-
ness of Scripture—and some are not comfortable with
even this—it has no place in a discussion of purgatory
where the soul is immersed in the love of God and any
pain derives "from the fact that my own guilt will
stand in unbearable contrast to the absolute love God
has for me,"[13] not from the ill-conceived idea that a sinner must pay for sin with suffering in an arbitrary way.

In heaven, the saved are not only immersed in the
love of God, but "in its corporate dimension, heaven

means the fulfillment of all relationships in the depth of the final relation with God."[14] "In heaven believers will have fellowship with God and with each other in a perfect environment" (Heb 12:22–23).[15]

It is, of course, this understanding of heaven as a "perfect environment" that has led to theologizing about postmortem purification. If we all entered heaven the way we left earth, it could be nothing like a "perfect environment." We will not, of course, enter heaven in such a way. Heaven is the unmitigated presence of God, as both traditions affirm. It is being with Christ. There is no hesitation, in either tradition, to affirm the fact that a relationship with Christ changes us. It is our weak and stubborn nature, our refusal to let grace permeate our lives, that slows the process of sanctification in this life. Such impediments cannot persist when we see the Lord face to face (1 Cor 13:12).[16] In this regard, the Catholic doctrine of purgatory affirms simply that the removal of such impediments will hurt, the more so the tighter our hold on them.

## Communion of Saints

Both Catholics and Evangelicals affirm belief in the Communion of Saints when they profess the Apostles' Creed. In the previous section it was demonstrated that both acknowledge a communal aspect of heaven. This means that those in the Body of Christ are in communion with each other, through the Holy Spirit (in whose section of the creed the Communion of Saints is found). Furthermore, all accounts agree that "the traditional, and probably the best, interpretation refers the phrase to the union of all believers, living or dead, in Christ, stressing their common life in Christ and their sharing of all the blessings of God."[17]

It has been established that prayer for the dead was a decisive contributing factor in the development of the doctrine of purgatory. It is the relationship between the Communion of Saints and the practice of prayer for the dead that is of interest for the theology of purgatory. Both Gouvea and G. L. B. specifically note that Catholicism justifies prayer for the dead with this article of the creed and that such a justification is unwarranted given its lack of biblical support.[18]

The biblical support for such a practice is admittedly minimal. Only two passages come to mind: the aforementioned passage from Maccabees that Evangelicals do not take to be part of the canon of Scripture, and the difficult suggestion of postmortem baptism in 1 Corinthians 15:29. It was mentioned earlier that the Maccabees passage can, at least, indicate an aspect of Jewish piety in the intertestamental period. Regardless of what one makes of the verse in Corinthians[19]—and neither Catholics nor Evangelicals practice postmortem baptisms—it seems at least clear that the Scriptures represent early Christians having a sense that death did not isolate individuals from the community.[20] It is an expression of the New Testament principle

60

that "the ultimate criteria is not biological but Christological; am I with Christ?"[21]

The evidence for prayer for the dead is, nevertheless, certainly more historical than biblical. Christians seem to always have prayed for the dead and all of the fathers strongly support this practice. Notably, none reject it.[22] It was an unquestioned element of the Christian patrimony in the East and West until the time of the Reformation.

John Campbell has written a fascinating article titled "Forgiveness in the Age to Come" (cf. Matt 12:32) in which he strongly attacks the Catholic doctrine of purgatory (as he understands it)[23] as "perhaps the grandest and most fantastical systematized error in the history of the Church."[24] Campbell's main point is that the heretical doctrine of purgatory, rightly rejected by the Reformers, has "engendered a deep suspicion of any teaching concerning accountability and judgment based on a believer's works or condition."[25] Since rejecting purgatory, those in the Reformation tradition have come to reject any possibility of postmortem suffering, a teaching that he sees as unambiguous in the New Testament and in the teachings of the church fathers.[26]

Campbell covers a lot of ground in his lengthy article. What is important here is that Campbell, while accepting the teachings of the fathers concerning postmortem purgation, including even the imagery of fire, dismisses their insistence on prayer for the dead as "a simple movement of misguided piety...that was in vogue among early Christians."[27]

Is it at least possible that Campbell is here making the same mistake that he accuses his coreligionists of with regards to postmortem purification? Is it possible that "the darkness and excesses of Catholic teaching and practice"[28] that made the Reformers and their heirs hesitant in affirming any suggestion of purgation is what makes Campbell, this time *with* his coreligionists, reject prayer for the dead?

Here it must be recognized that prayer for the dead is easily confused with prayer to the dead, and prayer to the dead is easily understood as idolatry. Furthermore, intercourse with the dead is strictly forbidden in the Old Testament as a form of divination. Prayer *for* the dead is prayer *to* God on behalf of another Christian who needs help. (If ever it has been construed in pious legends of Catholic culture as akin to divination, this is an abuse, and one that Catholics must work to prevent.) If our criteria are Christological and not biological, whether they are physically dead or not makes no difference. If it is accepted that such Christians exist (i.e., physically dead but still in need of aid), such prayer should pose little problem if we accept that those in the Body of Christ can aid one another by prayer.[29]

This problem is admittedly a difficult one. It is to be hoped that Catholics can so purify their relationships with the dead in Christ that any hint of divination or idolatry is not a factor in Evangelical critiques of this practice. On the other hand, it is to be hoped that Evangelicals will take the effort to evaluate this ancient, and until the Reformation universal,[30] Christian practice as it relates to the broader Christian truth that Christ has conquered death and that all in Christ are in communion with one another. Only in this way can their conclusions not be unfairly prejudiced by the abuses that occasioned the original rejection of the practice.

# Value of Suffering

Both Catholics and Evangelicals affirm, with Scripture, that suffering is part of God's plan of redemption. Paradigmatic, of course, is the suffering of Jesus Christ, of whom the author of the Letter to the Hebrews writes, "It was fitting that God, for whom and through whom all things exist, in bringing many children to glory, should make the pioneer of their salvation perfect through sufferings" (Heb 2:10). But Christ's sufferings do not make Christian suffering superfluous. Rather, Christians are called to participate in Christ's sufferings as Paul teaches in Romans 8:17, where he suggests suffering with Christ is a prerequisite for being glorified with him. This teaching in Romans gives the key for interpreting a very difficult passage in Colossians. Catholics and Evangelicals would agree that when Paul writes "I am now rejoicing in my sufferings for your sake, and in my flesh I am completing what is lacking in Christ's afflictions for the sake of his body, that is, the church" (Col 1:24), he is not teaching the insufficiency of Christ's sacrifice, but that we participate in Christ's suffering precisely as members of his body. The efficacy of Paul's suffering (and the same can be said of our own) is "not alongside of Christ, but *with* Christ working through Paul as a member of the body [emphasis added]."[31]

Indeed, the New Testament is clear that Christian suffering takes on new meaning in light of the cross. As Christ was brought to perfection by suffering (Heb 2:10), so are we who are called to imitate him. *The New Dictionary of Theology* entry for "Suffering" states that "Christians are saved *in* such suffering and not *from* it. They share with all mankind the experience of and vulnerability to it. The vital and spectacular difference is God's use of it and their response to it."[32] In a way this distinction is illustrative of the difference between pains that are "purgatorial" and the pains of damnation. Suffering apart from Christ is hell, and will be for eternity. Suffering with Christ leads to the complete transformation of the human person so as to be fit for the presence of God in heaven.

J. S. Feinberg gives a concise survey of how Scripture understands God's use of suffering in the lives of Christians:

According to Peter, suffering promotes sanctification (1 Pet 4:1–2). It does so in various ways such as refining the believer's faith (1 Pet 1:6–7), educating the believer in such Christian virtues as endurance and perseverance (Rom 5:3–4; James 1:3–4), teaching the believer something more of the sovereignty of God so that he understands his Lord better (Job 42:2–4), and giving the believer an opportunity to imitate Christ (1 Pet 3:17–18). If any of these occurs in the life of the believer, it will be evidence of sanctification, and such sanctification is worked through affliction.[33]

Fascinating, for a discussion of purgatory, is the fact that Scripture's "most common literary figure in regard to pain...is the pain of childbirth."[34] Romans 8:22 speaks of "the whole creation...groaning in labour pains." Scripture presents God's work of the new creation, both individual (Rom 8: 23) and universal, as being brought forth painfully. Given the instrumentality of the suffering of Christ in the genesis of that new creation, this should not be surprising.

Far from the suffering of our re-creation being a work that detracts from God's grace, "suffering can be the direct result of grace. Only Christians can experience the civil war of spirit and flesh, described by Paul in Galatians 5:17, and graphically personalized in Romans 7:14–25."[35] Reading these passages shows that Paul's *awareness* of his own sinfulness is both a gift of grace and a cause of suffering. This is entirely consistent with our reflections concerning the nature of the pain of purgatory.

> Paul interprets his own suffering as a means of ensuring that he be ever conscious of his own weakness, so that he remembers always that the power at work in him is from God and not himself and so that he is not deluded into relying on his own power (2 Cor 1:8–10; 4:7–12).[36]

Affirming the value of suffering in the Christian life should never be construed as works-righteousness whereby one's awareness of one's reliance on God is obscured. Perhaps by now it goes without saying that this admonition is meant both for Catholics and for Evangelicals.

The above teaching on suffering in the Christian worldview has been derived almost exclusively from Evangelical sources (the quote from Dulles, though it appears in an Evangelical publication, being the exception), but it seems entirely compatible with Catholic teaching on the suffering of purgatory. Again, as in the last section, the remaining issue is whether or not Christians can affirm the existence of "saved" souls who require some sanctification beyond what was made manifest in this life. Should the existence of such souls be affirmed, it is certainly not contrary to Scripture to affirm that suffering *with* Christ plays a role in their complete sanctification.

One final note is required in this section. Modern Catholic discourse regarding purgatory has moved away from any teaching regarding souls suffering expiatory pains.[37] While a careful study might demonstrate that the tradition did not mean, by affirming such sufferings, to compare them in efficacy to the expiatory sufferings of Christ, the trend away from such language is certainly to be applauded and encouraged. Regardless of the intricacies of the doctrine, using the same word to describe the effects of the sufferings of Christ and those of the souls in purgatory gives the wrong impression to both Catholics who accept purgatory and to other Christians who reject it. If the tradition is concerned about sins for which we have not yet appropriated God's grace and forgiveness—and it is—it is much better to speak, as Robert Ombres does, of a process "whereby the soul integrates its decision for God at all levels,"[38] than of expiating one's sins. This new language loses none of the value of the old because it still affirms that the remains of sin is what impedes the "decision for God," but it surpasses it by avoiding any sense that one does for oneself what can only be done by God on one's behalf.

# Presence of God

Both Catholics and Evangelicals affirm that the radical holiness of God is, apart from the work of Christ, unbearable to sinful humanity. God's very presence is, in itself, "a place of Judgment."[39] That nothing impure shall enter God's presence is obvious from the beginning of Genesis, when Adam and Eve hide because of their sinfulness (Gen 3:8),[40] to the end of Revelation, which proclaims that nothing unclean shall enter the eschatological city (Rev 21:27).[41]

"The Bible describes heaven as a place filled with God's presence."[42] As such, purity is the requirement of heaven. The New Testament is clear as to how this is to be achieved: through Christ. The Epistle of Jude glorifies "him who is able to keep you from falling, and to make you stand without blemish in the presence of his rejoicing" (Jude 1:24). Here is demonstrated not simply a forensic declared purity, but a real manifested purity. Bromiley writes that "we are received into God's eternal presence only as we have first received God present to us in Jesus Christ (John 1:12)."[43]

In this sense, purgatory can be understood as the full and final reception of Jesus Christ into any areas of our lives to which we have hitherto denied him access. Only Jesus is pure enough for heaven, but "what we do know is this: when he is revealed, we will be like him, for we will see him as he is" (1 John 3:2). What makes us, finally, "like" Jesus? Nothing but seeing face to face, fully knowing as we are fully known (1 Cor 13:12). The presence of God demands perfection but, it is the presence of God, in Christ, that effects our final perfection.[44]

# Christian Perfection

Both Catholic and Evangelicals affirm the Christian call to perfection as expressed in the exhortation of Jesus to "be perfect, therefore, as your heavenly Father is perfect" (Matt 5:48). The various Protestant traditions that influence modern Evangelicalism have pursued the question of Christian perfection. Some, Lutheran and Calvinist, deny that perfection is attainable in this life; others, notably Wesleyan, affirm that it is. None, however, suggests that *all* Christians attain perfection in this life. The term "perfection" has been understood to mean many, interrelated, things from imputed righteousness, to moral excellence, to a mature and authentic relationship with God. Regardless, the need for God's grace has been paramount in the Protestant tradition.[45] Perhaps Robert Yarbrough's contention that "believers are perfect to the extent that they participate in the cruciform grace that God offers in Christ,"[46] best captures the Evangelical position because it highlights the primacy of God's grace in the achievement of Christian perfection.

If this is so, it may be posited that believers will be perfect in heaven because in heaven they will fully participate in the grace offered in Christ, in the very life of Christ. The Catholic tradition suggests some have participated fully in this grace in this life and have had, therefore, no need of purgatory. The Evangelical tradition, with its many strands from various Protestant teachings, seems capable of affirming, at least, that many Christians die without having fully participated in the grace offered in Christ. This affirmation is, essentially, a restatement of the original theological problem that Catholics have answered with purgatory: many Christians seem to die without having been fully sanctified and made fit to inhabit heaven. Evangelicals, recognizing the need for perfection in the presence of God, have not ignored this problem. It is the purpose of the next chapter to study the way God's judgment—and his very presence *is* judgment—functions in Evangelical Christianity as a solution to the problem of not-yet-perfected Christians.

## Review Questions

1.  How does the nature of heaven relate to the theology of purgatory?

2.  How does the doctrine of the Communion of Saints frame the question of prayer for the dead?

3.  How does participation in Christ's suffering illuminate the idea of suffering as means of sanctification?

4.  How does the demand, and promise, of Christian perfection relate to the presence of God?

# Chapter 4
# PURGATORY AND THE THEOLOGY OF JUDGMENT

A few years ago, some Catholics and their Evangelical friends sat together in an establishment known for its quality live music, and as they waited for the band to take the stage, the discussion turned to theology, particularly the theology of purgatory. The standard assertions and rebuttals took place until something novel, at least in my experience, happened. One of the Evangelicals said something to the effect of, "Oh yes, I think we believe something like that happens at judgment day. If that's what you mean by purgatory, it's not so bad." This comment was the germ for much later thought and led, eventually, to this book. In my preparations for this book, I followed up on my friend's suggestion that if Evangelicals deal with the problems that Catholics address in their doctrine of purgatory at all, the place they must deal with them is in the context of their theology of judgment.

Now, it must be admitted that many of the "people

71

in the pews" do not, in fact, think the issue of imperfect people inhabiting heaven is a great theological problem.[1] For such people, the judgment is seen as quite a benign event. It is the place where *others* are judged while I, and others like me, will simply be told, "Well done, good and faithful servant. Enter into the joy prepared for you." This is typically not the result of having considered the problem carefully and determining that it is not, in fact, of much significance. It is more often simply a matter of never having had the problem brought to one's attention at all. In this respect Evangelicals often resemble their Catholic neighbors who, when asked about purgatory, will generally have very little to say.

An Evangelical scholar like Miroslav Volf would probably contend that the fact that this theological problem is not troubling to many in the Evangelical community is a not a product of the topic's own irrelevance but of that community's situation in North American suburbia.[2] Volf, a Croatian, has lived through a scenario where rival groups of Christians and Muslims had slaughtered one another. It is not surprising then, that Volf's highly acclaimed work has often focused on the topic of reconciliation. Furthermore, he has extended his reflections on this topic into his reflections on eschatology[3] because the basic problem that Catholics address by purgatory is glaringly apparent to him, though in a slightly different form. For Volf, the question, "How can heaven be heaven given the fact that Christians are seen to die in a state of imperfection?" takes its strongest meaning in the formulation, "How can heaven be heaven given the fact that Christians are seen to die in enmity, even at war, with their fellow Christians?"[4] Indeed, it is precisely in human relationships where the imperfections of human persons are made most obviously manifest.

As already noted, many churchgoers have not examined the problem systematically. Volf notes that "popular piety is also aware of the issue. In tightly knit Christian communities, one sometimes hears the injunction that their members had better learn to love each other now since they will spend eternity together."[5] Despite this awareness, Volf is right to suggest that this is "an inadequately addressed theological issue."[6] Volf's conclusion is essential to my project. He writes:

> Sometime between a shadowy history and an eternity bathed in light, somewhere between this world and the coming world of perfect love, a transformation of persons and their complex relationships needs to take place. Without such transformation the world to come would not be a world of perfect love but only a repetition of a world in which, at best, the purest of loves falter and, at worst, cold indifference reigns and deadly hatreds easily flare up.[7]

And, following my Evangelical colleague's initial inspiring comments, Volf places this transformation at the last judgment.[8]

Though understood in traditional Catholic formulations as discrete events,[9] purgatory and judgment have never been far removed. In reflecting on the final destiny of the human person, St. Augustine wrote that God is "the Last Thing of the creature. Gained, He is its paradise; lost, He is its hell; as demanding, He is its judgment; as cleansing He is its purgatory."[10] God both requires perfection and achieves it in us. Judgment and purgatory are two sides of the same coin. Augustine speculated that the fire in the 1 Corinthians passage so important for the doctrine of purgatory could be understood as either purgative, part of the final judgment, or symbolic of the trials of daily life.[11] In light of the current understanding of purgatory, there is no reason why these alternatives need to be seen as exclusive at all. One could affirm all three. Even the element of fire, so controversially attached to the doctrine of purgatory, has its scriptural origins as a metaphor of God's judgment.[12]

Since the rejection of purgatory in the sixteenth century, the doctrine of judgment has often been presented in a paradoxical way. Scripture seems to affirm two things about the judgment that are difficult to assert together without something at least *like* purgatory. The first is that Christians can approach the judgment with hope; the second is that the judgment is very severe. While Catholicism may be reproached for having focused too much on the latter, any Evangelicals who expect nothing more of the judgment for themselves than a welcome into heaven have certainly missed something essential.[13]

Willingdale blames this inconsistency in Protestant judgment theology on an overemphasis on forensic language in the early reformers. He notes that "since both the doctrines of justification and the Last Judgment were stated forensically rather than morally, the acquittal pronounced in the former left nothing to be declared at the latter, beyond the negative condemnation of the ungodly."[14] The result, for many modern Evangelicals, is a belief in a severe judgment, as taught in Scripture,[15] that is basically content-less. There is a vague idea that the severity of the judgment should keep Christians accountable, but given the lack of reflection on how the judgment might actually play out for a saved—but obviously unsanctified—person, the concept lacks substance.

Reflections like those of Volf go a long way toward imbuing Evangelical affirmations of the severity of judgment with substance. Volf insists on the fullness of Christian hope in Christ *and* a judgment that takes seriously what it means for sinful humanity to encounter the living God (Heb 10: 31).[16] As such, his work is extremely valuable for this project. We must now, accordingly, devote our energies to an investigation of Volf's theology of the last judgment.

# Volf's Theology of the Last Judgment

One of the ways in which the paradox in judgment theology has been manifested is in the struggle to reconcile the biblical teaching that judgment is according to works[17] with the Reformation emphasis on justification by faith.[18] Volf's reponse to this problem is elegant. He suggests that the confusion results from a simple misunderstanding as to the proper objects of the verbs "justify" and "judge." Persons are the proper object of justification; works, the proper object of judgment.[19] That this is so becomes clear if we try to imagine the reverse; that is, if we try to imagine having our works justified before God.[20] This is not to say we are entirely independent of our works. They do, in fact, manifest our character.[21] We can see the wisdom of Volf's solution, however, if we consider what we will take with us to heaven. Our persons *must* be there with us; our works need not be. Indeed, our evil works cannot be. They are instances of when we are less than ourselves, but in heaven we will be fully ourselves.[22]

For Volf, in order for our evil deeds to be excluded from heaven, they must be dealt with at the judgment. In heaven our sins will be forgiven and forgotten[23]—*in that order*. In order for sins to be forgiven, they must be acknowledged.[24] In his most famous work, *Exclusion and Embrace*, Volf writes:

> We seriously misconstrue forgiveness...if we understand it as acting "as if the sin was not

there."...There can be no redemption unless the truth about the world is told and justice is done. To treat sin as if it were not there, when in fact it is there, amounts to living as if the world were redeemed when in fact it is not.[25]

Volf's major contribution to the theology of judgment is his concern for healing human relationships of sin and its effects so that heaven can be heaven. For this reason he insists that the judgment will be accompanied by the "Final Reconciliation."[26] And here, just as our receiving forgiveness from God requires acknowledgment of our sins before God, "reconciliation between human beings cannot proceed...in disregard of justice; it rather requires that the claims of justice be recognized as valid and respected."[27] He echoes other voices in his tradition when he insists that "Judgement of grace is no lenient judgment."[28] He continues:

It is important not to set grace in opposition to justice. Grace does not negate justice; grace affirms justice while at the same time transcending its claims. The judgment of grace is a demanding judgment. It does not measure our behavior simply against justice but against grace. The crucial question will not be, "Have you followed the rules?" but "Have you shown mercy?" (Matt. 18 and 25).[29]

The great value of Volf is that he goes on to posit what this judgment will look like for those of us (that is, it seems, virtually all of us) who do not meet the lofty standards of the "judgment of grace." The common sentiment that Jesus takes care of it is, of course, entirely true and, often, entirely vacuous. "How does Jesus take care of it?" is the question that needs an answer.

To understand Volf's answer we first need to recognize his understanding of sin as a *social* reality. It is true that "though all sin is by definition sin against God, most of our sins are committed in dealings with others."[30] Furthermore, the complex web of human relationships means that it is impossible to identify individuals entirely as victims or perpetrators. We are all victims and we are all perpetrators. In fact, the logic of sin is such that victims are frequently turned into perpetrators by having been victimized, though they are often unable to recognize their own sin in the face of the horrors committed against them.[31] As such, everyone at the judgment will need both to forgive and to be forgiven.[32]

In his article "The Final Reconciliation," Volf offers us the best summary of his thought on this issue that I have been able to find. Here he provides a concise outline of what such reconciliation at the judgment would look like:

First, the reconciling event would not apply to some crimes of some people but to any (social) sin of any person; it would include all injustices, deceptions, and violences, whether miniscule or grand, whether committed intentionally or not, and whether the perpetrators were conscious of them or not. As a result, a clear division between the group of perpetrators and the group of victims would be broken, yet without blunting a sharp condemnation of the evil committed. Second, the judge as the third party would not simply define and set the process in motion but would, in the precise function of a judge who suffered the victim's fate and was judged in the perpetrator's place, be at the center of their reconciliation. Third, reconciliation between perpetrator and victim would be de-coupled from its necessary relation to the pain of the perpetrator, except for the pain of remorse; healing would be ascribed to the power of God's Spirit working through the display of truth and grace. Fourth, transformation of both perpetrators and victims would be affirmed; perpetrators would be liberated from their sin and (likely?) attempts at self-justification, and victims from their pain and (possible?) bitterness and vindictiveness.[33]

It would be unfair to Volf not to emphasize that all of this is accomplished in the context of grace. The full disclosure of all our failings and the recognition of the full humanity of our enemies, heretofore denied by us, would be a shattering reality were we not "freed from the guilt and transformed by that same Christ who has already become [our] 'righteousness and sanctification' (1 Cor 1:30)."[34]

By now at least some basic parallels with the doctrine of purgatory should be apparent. Volf certainly affirms the necessity of postmortem change in what he calls the "eschatological transition."[35] "Post-mortem change is an essential precondition for the resolution of the problems within the sphere of cultural productivity; without it past cannot be redeemed and history cannot be set aright."[36] To complete our task we must now investigate Volf's work in the light of the Catholic teaching about purgatory in order to ascertain what the two traditions may be able to affirm in common.

The first thing to note here is that both the Catholic and Evangelical traditions affirm that there may be human persons who have so oriented their souls *during this life* as to resist postmortem change. That is, there may be people who reject God's judgment and instead choose to exist apart from God and the community that is heaven. The language the Catholic Church has used to describe such people is that of "mortal sin." This is easily misunderstood when presented without nuance. It gives the impression that certain sins get one condemned to hell while others do not. The point is not that some sins, known as venial, don't separate us from God, but rather that some acts are so evil that to commit them with full knowledge and consent amounts to a complete rejection of God's grace. It affirms Jesus' claim that "Not everyone who says to me, 'Lord, Lord,' will enter the kingdom of heaven, but only one who does the will of my Father in heaven" (Matt 7:21). Volf's description of this hypothetical choice against God looks surprisingly like the Catholic concept of mortal sin. He advises that, "we should not, however, shy away from the unpleasant and deeply tragic *possibility* that there *might* be human beings, created in the image of God, who, through the practice of evil, have immunized themselves from all attempts at their redemption."[37] Catholics and Evangelicals both know that Scripture teaches that faith is more than mere intellectual assent to the proposal "Jesus is Lord." Such assent is given in the moral choices of one's life as well. That the "practice of evil," as Volf describes it, can lead to and manifest one's rejection of God is a reality that both traditions accept.

Those who go through purgatory, that is, those who accept God's judgment on their sin, do not reject God's gift. The reader will recall that in chapter 1 purgatory was presented as a solution to the question of Christians who died without having been fully sanctified.[38] Interestingly, Volf writes that "the last judgment is the final justification,"[39] and the language of his eschatology reflects justification more than sanctification. The Catholic tradition has not typically separated justification and sanctification the way the Protestant tradition has. Nevertheless, sanctification seems more related to the process of purgatory than does justification.

In "Enter into Joy," Volf declines to address the issue, writing that he "can leave aside here the important question about whether one should understand the last judgment as the completion of justification or sanctification."[40] This sentence is followed by a fascinating footnote. In it Volf informs us that

> in a formal response to this paper, Gregor Etzelmüller, building on Schleiemacher's reflections and on a reinterpretation of Karl Barth, rightly suggested that it may be better to conceive of the last judgment as the completion of sanctification rather than of justification.[41]

Unfortunately, Professor Etzelmüller's paper is not publicly available. Nevertheless, it is clear that Volf accepts Etzelmüller's proposal and does not see it as substantially altering his argument. As such, the Catholic view that purgatory completes our sanctification is not at odds with Volf's teaching that "divine judgment at the end of history completes divine justification."[42] Indeed, it seems both dialogue partners could agree[43] with the general outline that "the Christian life is a process which begins in justification, is actualized in sanctification, and is consummated with salvation."[44]

If both traditions can affirm that the justification/sanctification dynamic is not completed in this life, but only by the final encounter with the living God, much progress has been made toward removing the doctrine of purgatory as a stumbling block to unity.[45] In this light we can now investigate the important characteristics of the doctrine of purgatory to see what parallels may be found between Catholic teaching and the proposals of Professor Volf.

Perhaps purgatory's most salient feature is its association with pain and suffering. Cardinal Ratzinger insists that it cannot be understood as "some kind of supraworldly concentration camp where man is forced to undergo punishment in a more or less arbitrary fashion. Rather it is the inwardly necessary process of transformation in which a person becomes capable of Christ."[46] Volf, the reader will recall, allows in his formulation only "the pain of remorse."[47] This may initially seem like a setback, but a further investigation of Volf's work will allow us to perceive that it does no violence to his thought to interpret this "remorse" quite broadly. In the same article, Volf suggests that "Protestant theology has emphasized transformation as a sheer gift of God involving no other suffering than the pain of self-discovery."[48] This begins to flesh things out, for self-discovery precedes, if not temporally, at least logically, remorse. Furthermore, remorse is of little use if it does not lead to change. Can this change hurt? Remember that for Volf what is essential at the judgment is that one both give and accept forgiveness. Accepting forgiveness means, first of all, confessing guilt. In *Exclusion and Embrace*, Professor Volf suggests that both the confession of guilt and the forgiveness of the guilty are difficult and painful.[49] He even writes that "forgiveness itself is a form of suffering,"[50] because one is forgoing one's claim to strict justice in the recognition that, as Mother Teresa so pointedly put it, "An eye for an eye makes the world blind."[51]

Through this suffering, of giving and receiving forgiveness, we move beyond the hold that sin has on our lives and relationships so that we, victims and perpetrators all, can inhabit heaven as heaven. Interestingly, the mystics tell us that this experience, understood as purgatory, will be a strange mingling of suffering and joy. Volf comes to a similar conclusion. After our self-discovery, remorse, and giving and receiving forgiveness, all painful in their own ways, we will finally and completely end our association with sin by forgetting it. Volf writes, "enveloped in God's glory we will redeem ourselves and our enemies by one final act of *the most difficult grace made easy by the experience of salvation* that cannot be undone—the grace of nonremembering [emphasis added]."[52] Indeed, it is this experience of salvation, the knowledge of being safe in God's love, that the mystics tell us lends the pain of purgatory its sweetness. For Volf, that same experience makes the difficulty of reconciliation easy.

This leads us to the discussion of another paradox. In purgatory there is no chance of rejecting God's grace. It has been insisted that this is not a place of second chances but is rather the process of perfection for those who have already and definitively chosen God as their ultimate good. Nevertheless, one of the reasons purgatory seems necessary is that it is not satisfactory that we should be magically transformed, so as to be able to inhabit heaven, with no accession to such a process on our part.[53] We must appropriate God's grace. As in this life, what remains for us is the simple, if not easy, acceptance of God's gracious love. The same holds true for the reconciliation Volf posits at the judgment. He insists that, "as a transition to the world of perfect love, the last judgment is unthinkable without its *appropriation* by persons on whom it is effected."[54] In another place he writes that "[t]he last judgment conceived of as the final justification presupposes persons as active recipients of divine grace."[55] This dynamic has been captured in the pithy statement of Luther, who rightly noted that God "does not work in us without us."[56]

## Process of Healing

How is the change effected in us? Volf has suggested that "healing would be ascribed to the power of

God's Spirit working through the display of truth and grace."[57] It is certainly the third person of the Trinity who is given the name Healer. It is the second, however, who claimed that "I am the Truth." It is the encounter with this truth, an encounter with Christ, the judge who suffered *as* the victim and *for* the perpetrator and who offers the grace of forgiveness that underlies the possibility for the healing in the Holy Spirit. As noted earlier, discovery precedes the remorse that precedes the change in the human person. In Christ we will discover the truth about ourselves and our relationships with others.

Volf has rightly insisted that reconciliation with God is impossible without reconciliation with one another. He notes that, were this not the case, Jesus' injunction in Matthew 5:23–24[58] to reconcile with one's brothers and sisters before approaching the altar would be nonsense.[59] Indeed, the eschatological transition must "be understood not only as a divine act toward human beings but also as *a social event between human beings*, more precisely, a divine act toward human beings which is also a social event between them."[60] Gabriel Fackre expresses the idea this way: "to see in the Light is to see *by* the light. Vertical and horizontal relationships are inseparable. The radiance of God opens our eyes to the others who surround the throne."[61]

That the relationship with one's fellow creatures is given such prominence in Volf's eschatology is certainly promising. The reader will recall that important aspects of the doctrine of purgatory are located specifically in the Catholic understanding of the Communion of Saints. In "Love Your Heavenly Enemy," Volf points out that "not even the Roman Catholic doctrine of purgatory compellingly addresses the *social* aspect of the transformation that needs to happen if we are to inhabit the world of love."[62] This is one of the rare times where Volf mentions purgatory, but it demonstrates that he is not unaware of some of the overlap between the concerns he is addressing with his work and the concerns Catholicism addresses by its doctrine of purgatory. What are we to make of his claim that purgatory does not address the social aspect he is concerned with in a satisfactory way?

The answer here is twofold. First of all, the relations between Christians are fundamental to the doctrine of purgatory, and so the resources to address Volf's concerns are available within the Catholic tradition. Secondly, it must be admitted that, even with the focus on the Communion of Saints in relation to purgatory, Catholicism has not emphasized and articulated the need for postmortem reconciliation that Volf convincingly argues is necessary.

Catholicism certainly accepts the assertion that to be in communion with God is to be in communion with everyone else who is in communion with God. It is perhaps this overwhelming conviction that has led to Catholicism's lack of reflection in the area of Volf's concern. The Catholic tradition *assumes* that becoming perfected so as to live with God entails a perfection of relationships with others. Fackre's contention that seeing God means seeing everything about our relationships with others in the light of truth is entirely compatible with Catholic sensibilities about purgatory.

If Catholicism already accepts, at least implicitly, the notions that underlay Volf's work on reconciliation, is there anything that Catholics can learn from this encounter with Evangelical thought? I believe there is. In the first instance, spelling out concretely what was only implied before is certainly an advantage. Beyond that, however, Volf's reflections can aid the Catholic tradition in at least two ways.

# Reconciliation with Others

In chapter 3, it was suggested that, as a means toward unity on the issue of prayer for the dead, Catholics need to purify their relationships with the dead so that nothing superstitious, magical, or mechanical can be ascertained in their practices regarding prayers for the faithful departed. In this regard, Volf's insistence that part of what is necessary for heaven to be heaven is that those in the Body of Christ be reconciled, can imbue Catholic piety vis-à-vis the dead with a sense of responsibility for reconciliation. In chapter 1, consideration was given to the problem of what prayer for the dead can actually accomplish. It cannot be the case that certain prayers or sufferings are equivalent to a given amount of "time" in purgatory. The person must be perfected and there is no substitute for that. However, if part of being perfected means being reconciled with others, then Catholics can attach to their prayers a sincere examination of conscience regarding their relationship with the dead person, and try to embody the giving and acceptance of forgiveness with them in this life and in this way anticipate the judgment. What Volf rightly notes when he claims that "reflection on the great transition from the present world to the world to come is always already reflection on many small transitions within the present world,"[63] holds true across the whole range of Christian eschatology.

The second area where Volf's reflections seem helpful is in reconciling some new voices in the tradition with the mainstream of Catholic reflection regarding purgatory. Purgatory is typically understood as a process for sinners, that is, perpetrators, to be perfected. In recent years, Catholic theologians have speculated on the possibility of postmortem healing for those who were so severely victimized in this life as to have had no opportunity to make a genuine choice for God.[64] If such speculations were to be taken to the extreme, these new formulations could take the form of offering a second chance for salvation after death. I suggest that the Catholic tradition cannot support such extremes.[65] Further, it will not help ecumenical dialogue if some in the Catholic tradition seem to teach a

second chance for salvation after death while others
are busy insisting to their separated brethren that we
do not, in fact, understand purgatory as a second
chance. It is nevertheless important to acknowledge
that the problems mentioned by these theologians are
not negligible. There are people so victimized in this
life that it is difficult to imagine a just and loving God
not offering an opportunity for healing.

Volf's elucidations regarding the relationships
between victim and perpetrator, especially in *Exclusion
and Embrace*,[66] may offer a way forward in this situation. The social reconciliation he imagines allows the
victim the grace of forgiving the perpetrator and of
having the perpetrator's deeds acknowledged and condemned before all creation. Both these aspects seem
essential to the healing of the victim. Furthermore,
though examples are imaginable where the victim is
entirely innocent, Volf points out that in the vast
majority of cases the line between victim and perpetrator is drawn within human persons and not
between them. Volf's focus on *relationships* helps us to
overcome the dichotomy between a purgatory (often
seen in terms of punishment) for perpetrators and a
purgatory (seen in terms of healing) for victims. We
will all have our sins judged and we will all have our
wounds healed, for heaven can abide neither.

# Review Questions

1.  How do purgatory and the last judgment relate to reconciliation between Christians?

2.  Do you think Professor Volf's proposals would be acceptable to Catholics? To Evangelicals?

3.  How do Volf's ideas help us to understand purgatory as affecting both sinners and victims?

# CONCLUSION
*"Jesus Is Our Purgatory"*

In the course of researching this book , a Google search brought me to JustForCatholics.org, a website that does not view Catholics as dialogue partners or fellow Christians, but simply as potential converts to "biblical Christianity." Such organizations are not typically interested in contributing to ecumenical dialogue.[1] Remarkably, in the section devoted to purgatory, the following assertion is made: "Jesus Christ, and nothing else, is our purification, our purgatory."[2] Excitedly, I wrote an e-mail to Dr. Joe Mizzi, who had written the article, and informed him that his statement had captured the essence of Catholic doctrine on the subject and that we were not as far apart as he supposed. My hopes were short lived as he promptly informed me that Catholics do not, in fact, believe that Jesus is their purgatory and invited me to join him in his mission to present Catholics with the truth about what they believe. What should be encouraging to ecumenists is that, even as Dr. Mizzi explicitly rejects both ecumenism generally and the particular claims of Catholics concerning what they actually believe, he is willing to conclude his article about purgatory by writing: "Do you believe in purgatory? I hope you will affirm, 'Yes, I believe in God's purgatory. My purgatory is the Lord Jesus Christ!'"[3]

If the proposal that "Jesus is our purgatory" is acceptable to Evangelical Christians, it will only be those who dismiss ecumenical dialogue in principle who continue to view purgatory as a barrier to communion. It is a hopeful circumstance that no less a representative of the Catholic tradition than Joseph Ratzinger, the current Pope Benedict XVI, comes to essentially the same conclusion as Dr. Mizzi's pithy phrase in his work *Death and Eternal Life*.[4] He writes that "purgatory is understood in a properly Christian way when it is grasped Christologically, in terms of the Lord himself as the judging fire which transforms us and conforms us to his own glorified body."[5]

Here again, we note the proximity between the idea of purgatory and that of judgment. Jesus is the "judging fire." Eberhard Jüngel, in his article "The Last Judgment as an Act of Grace," insists that foundational to any Christian theology of judgment is the identity of the judge.[6] Indeed, "to be judged by Christ is a *blessing* which befalls humanity."[7] In the judgment, "our sin and guilt is revealed with an unsurpassed clarity in the person of Jesus Christ,"[8] but it is also in him that they are overcome. Christ is our judge and Christ is our purgatory!

This book will not presume to have definitively solved the problem of purgatory as a disputed doctrine between Christians of various denominations. Nevertheless, it is hoped that the engagement with Evangelical judgment theology has indicated that ideas such as postmortem change, pain at the revealing of one's sinful life, and need for the "consummation" of one's relationship with God and others is not incoherent to Evangelical Christianity. It seems then that, for the most part, the aspects of purgatory to which Evangelicals object are either aspects to which Catholics also object or that are, at least, not central to the doctrine.

The notable exception to this statement is, of course, prayer for the dead. I have suggested earlier that it would serve the dialogue well for Evangelicals to honestly question their own tradition to discern whether prayer for the dead was rejected on its own merits or if it was simply the baby thrown out with the proverbial bathwater of abuses that surrounded the doctrine of purgatory.[9] I now want to add the observation that, even if Evangelicals feel that they can in no way accommodate prayer for the dead in their tradition,[10] they should not see it as a barrier to communion with Roman Catholics for the simple reason that they do not see it as a barrier for their communion with the earliest Christians.[11] It is true that prayer for the dead is not endorsed in the New Testament, but it is also true that those communities responsible for producing the New Testament undoubtedly prayed for the dead and that nowhere in the correspondence that has come down to us as sacred Scripture or in other documents of the early church is this practice condemned. It is, in fact, clear from many passages in the New Testament that the earliest Christian communities understood Christ's victory over death to imply that the question of what permitted communion between human persons was not being biologically dead or alive, but being with Christ or not.[12]

Another note that must be made is that this book has avoided the debates concerning the "timing" of the last things. In some circles the precise order of eschatological events is the cause of much debate and even division. Within Catholicism itself, purgatory has been presented, though never definitively, as taking place prior to the last judgment. Furthermore, I have not delved at all into the details regarding the particular and final judgments.[13] It is my position that, while such concerns may not be inconsequential, they do not affect the basic premise of this work, that is, that Catholics and Evangelicals recognize similar theological problems regarding the death of imperfect Christians and have come up with complementary, rather than contradictory, responses to this problem. *The Evangelical New Dictionary of Theology* notes that, in many matters eschatological, "Scripture seems to describe what is beyond our experience in terms of the limitations of our experience of temporal distinctions."[14]

Whether or not Evangelicals adopt the doctrine of

purgatory, the appropriation of a secondary Christian doctrine is not what is necessary for the unity of the church. Rather, what is hoped is that the doctrine of purgatory is recognized as a coherent Christian response to a genuine theological problem and not seen merely as a stereotypical example of Catholic perversion of the gospel. Should this be achieved even in small groups, goodwill regarding further ecumenical dialogue with the Catholic Church will be fostered in Evangelical circles. Furthermore, among Catholics, a renewed understanding of this doctrine encourages practices consistent with the gospel, and a heightened awareness of the impact of the encounter of Christ with the human person.

## Christ Is Our Unity

John 3:19–20 offers the most concise theology of the judgment in the Scriptures. "This is the judgment, that the light has come into the world, and men loved darkness rather than light, because their deeds were evil. For everyone who does evil hates the light, and does not come to the light, lest his deeds be exposed." In the quest for Christian unity, the theology of judgment and of purgatory provides us with a salutary model. The root of our division is sin. The good news is that Christ has promised to work in us to deliver us from that sin and its consequences. When we come before the light of Christ and let our deeds be exposed, we are vulnerable, but we are forgiven and healed.

As each of the Christian denominations seeks unity with its brethren, let it submit to the judgment of Christ. Let them undergo the purification that a radical encounter with the risen Lord entails. It has often been said that as we grow closer to him we grow, inevitably, closer to each other. This is made apparent in a new and startling way when viewed in the light of the insights of purgatory and the last judgment. A careful investigation of these doctrines has shown that there is no escaping the call to reconciliation without a rejection of God, God's judgment, and God's promise to perfect us. In this creation that is continually being refined by the love of God, Jesus is our purgatory, Jesus is our judge, Jesus is our unity!

## Review Questions

1. Should the claim "Jesus is our purgatory" be acceptable to Catholics and Evangelicals? Why or why not?

2. Are any remaining differences over purgatory or prayer for the dead serious enough to justify the division of the church?

3. How does a purgatorial spirituality inform the quest for Christian unity?

# NOTES

## Introduction

1. Though the original and explicit goal of this work is to investigate the doctrine of purgatory as a topic of dialogue between Catholics and Evangelical Protestants, I am aware that the term "Evangelical" is difficult to define, and it is not always clear why the term "Evangelical" would be used rather than simply "Protestant." Though most of the Protestant sources for this book were Evangelical sources, it seems clear to me that the conclusions reached here are broadly applicable to other communities who trace their roots to the Reformation. Significantly, Miroslav Volf, the Evangelical scholar I engage in chapter 4, is notable for the way in which he is able to represent both classical Protestantism and the Evangelical community. The interested reader might peruse Volf's own bibliographies to gain an appreciation for Volf's engagement with the broader, particularly Lutheran, Protestant tradition.

2. I make no claims to this having been a scientifically accurate survey and fully recognize the limitations of this methodology. My decision to pursue this course was based on the fact that any evidence I had of Evangelical attitudes toward purgatory was quite anecdotal: conversations with

friends and the perusal of antiCatholic literature that may or may not represent the thought of most Evangelicals. There is little academic work on this topic.

3. Robert Ombres, *The Theology of Purgatory* (Dublin: Mercier Press, 1980), 47.

4. Joseph Ratzinger, *Eschatology: Death and Eternal Life*, Dogmatic Theology (Washington DC: The Catholic University of America Press, 1988), 233; Jerome R. Dollard, "Eschatology: A Roman Catholic Perspective," *Review and Expositor* 79 (1982): 374.

5. "Jesus knew that they wanted to ask him, so he said to them, 'Are you discussing among yourselves what I meant when I said, "A little while, and you will no longer see me, and again a little while, and you will see me"? Very truly, I tell you, you will weep and mourn, but the world will rejoice; you will have pain, but your pain will turn into joy. When a woman is in labor, she has pain, because her hour has come. But when her child is born, she no longer remembers the anguish because of the joy of having brought a human being into the world. So you have pain now; but I will see you again, and your hearts will rejoice, and no one will take your joy from you.'" (This and all further biblical quotations are taken from the New Revised Standard Version of the Bible.)

6. Ombres, *The Theology of Purgatory*, 13.

7. See, for example, David Brown, "No Heaven without Purgatory," *Religious Studies* 21, no. 4 (December 1985): 447–56; Brian L. Horne, "Where Is Purgatory?" in *"If Christ Be Not Risen"* (San Francisco: Collins Liturgical, 1988), 92–100; Jerry L. Walls, "Purgatory for Everyone," *First Things* 122 (April 2002): 26–30.

8. A small burst of material followed the publication of Jacques Le Goff, *The Birth of Purgatory* (Chicago: University

of Chicago Press, 1984), but these sources are more histori-cal than theological.

9. See, for example, Bernhard Bartmann, *Purgatory: A Book of Christian Comfort* (London: Burns Oates & Washbourne, Ltd, 1936); Mother Mary of St. Austin, *The Divine Crucible of Purgatory* (New York: P. J. Kenedy & Sons, 1940).

10. Ombres, *The Theology of Purgatory*, 7. See also L. Stafford Betty, "The Great Chain of Being in the Lives of the Faithful: The Status of Purgatory Today," in *Fragments of Infinity* (Dorset, UK: Prism, 1991), 21–30.

11. It is hoped that the reader will forgive the length of the following quote on the premise that its length and detail is part of what needs illustrating.

12. F. X. Shouppe, *Purgatory: Illustrated by the Lives and Legends of the Saints* (Rockford, IL: Tan Books and Publishers, Inc., 1973), 69.

13. Horne, "Where Is Purgatory?" 98.

14. H. A. Reinhold, "All That Rest in Christ," *Worship* 26, no. 6 (May 1952): 302.

15. Betty, "The Great Chain of Being," 23.

# Chapter 1

1. Ratzinger, *Eschatology*, 233.

2. The Orthodox, it should be noted, do not subscribe to the Western belief, and even pray for the souls in hell.

3. Anglicans occasionally affirm the value of prayer for the dead. See, for example, Anglican-Orthodox Dialogue, "The Communion of Saints and the Departed," *Sobornost* 3 (1981): 95.

4. See, for example, Miroslav Volf, "Reconciled in the End," *Christian Century* 116 (1999): 1098.

5. Ratzinger, *Eschatology*, 230–31.

6. See, for example, Le Goff, *The Birth of Purgatory*, 73, and the subsequent discussion in Graham Edwards, "Purgatory: 'Birth' or Evolution," *Journal of Ecclesiastical History* 36, no. 4 (October 1985): 640–42.

7. Ombres, *The Theology of Purgatory*, 11.

8. Reinhold, "All That Rest in Christ," 300.

9. It is interesting to note that, in the e-mail survey mentioned above, some Evangelicals gave evidence of believing some of the following misconceptions about purgatory, while others were careful to note in their answers that "Purgatory is not, like many of my fellow evangelicals think...." This awareness in many members of the Evangelical community is encouraging and probably evidence of, at least, informal dialogue between Evangelicals and Catholics on a grassroots level.

10. Robert Ombres, "The Doctrine of Purgatory According to St. Thomas Aquinas," *Downside Review* 99 (October 1981): 283.

11. Ron Rolheiser, *Purgatory Leads the Dead Soul to Heaven* (2003), http://www.wcr.ab.ca/columns/rolheiser/2003/rolheiser120103.shtml.

12. R.T.D., "Purgatory," in *New Dictionary of Theology*, ed. J. I. Packer, Sinclair B. Ferguson, and David F. Wright (Downer's Grove, IL: InterVarsity Press, 1988), 549.

13. Another common formulation, that purgatory is a state between earth and heaven, is closer to the meaning of the doctrine, though I believe there are better ways to express this.

14. J. P. Arendzen, *Purgatory and Heaven* (New York: Sheed and Ward, 1960), 29–31; Ombres, *The Theology of*

*Purgatory*, 76–77. For this reason, Robert Ombres suggests the Catholic Church curtail any discussion of the *poena damni* as constituent of purgatory. See Ombres, *The Theology of Purgatory*, 75. I heartily second this proposal.

15. Larissa Juliet Taylor, "God of Judgment, God of Love: Catholic Preaching in France, 1460–1560," *Historical Reflections* 26, no. 2 (2000): 255.

16. Dollard, "Eschatology," 374.

17. An attempt to write an ecumenically sensitive treatment of the doctrine of purgatory can look like apologetics. This is not the intention here. Rather, it is hoped that in the doctrine so presented, Evangelicals can recognize facets of a faith they already hold articulated in new, and it is hoped, helpful ways. If Christian denominations are ever to change doctrinal positions in the quest for unity, it must happen from the inside. The work of ecumenism focuses, rather, on discovering what we hold in common. It is when we can recognize the other's faith as authentically Christian that the insights of our brethren may challenge us to a fuller faith.

18. Though no official teaching is available, or even appropriate, most reflections on purgatory seem to presume that those who are not perfected at death are in the majority.

19. Evangelical theologian Miroslav Volf rightly points out that "reflection on the great transition from the present world to the world to come is always already reflection on many small transitions within the present world. See Miroslav Volf, "Enter into Joy! Sin, Death, and the Life of the World to Come," in *End of the World and the Ends of God* (Harrisburg, PA: Trinity Press International, 2000), 259.

20. Walls, "Purgatory for Everyone," 27.

21. Ratzinger, *Eschatology*, 230.

22. Ombres, *The Theology of Purgatory*, 63.

23. Brown, "No Heaven without Purgatory."

24. Ibid., 450–51.

25. I recommend that the interested reader seek out this article and peruse this and Brown's other arguments in their entirety.

26. Brown, "No Heaven without Purgatory," 451–53.

27. Horne, "Where Is Purgatory?" 98.

28. "The Gift of Salvation," an ecumenical document signed by Evangelicals and Catholics, affirms salvation as not simply forgiveness, but what Walls calls "also a matter of thorough moral and spiritual transformation." Walls, "Purgatory for Everyone," 26.

29. Dorothy L. Sayers, "Introduction to The *Comedy* of Dante Alighieri the Florentine," in *The* Comedy *of Dante Alighieri the Florentine, Cantica II: Purgatory* (Harmondsworth: Penguin Books, 1981), 57.

30. Indeed, as Robert Ombres notes, that language has been removed from the new Order for the Sacrament of Penance. See Ombres, "The Doctrine of Purgatory," 68.

31. See R. E. O. White, "Sanctification," in *Evangelical Dictionary of Theology, Second Edition*, ed. Walter A. Elwell (Grand Rapids, MI: Baker Academic, 2001), 1052. This Evangelical author uses the language of "status conferred" and "process pursued" to capture essentially the same idea.

32. Augustine of Hippo, "On the Trinity: Book Eight, Chapter 17," in *Augustine of Hippo: Selected Writings*, ed. Mary T. Clark (New York: Paulist Press, 1984), 356.

33. Again, Volf is helpful. He notes that "[e]verything has already been accomplished *de jure* in Christ (to use Karl Barth's favorite way of putting it), and whatever still remains to be done so that it would be realized also *de facto*, is an unfailing divine work." See Miroslav Volf, "The Final

Reconciliation: Reflections on a Social Dimension of the Eschatological Transition," *Modern Theology* 16, no. 1 (January 2000): 104.

34. Brown, "No Heaven without Purgatory," 453.

35. Sayers, "Introduction to The Comedy of Dante Alighieri the Florentine," 55–59.

36. John Paul II, "General Audience," in *General Audience, Wednesday 4 August 1999* (1999), http://www.vatican.va/holy_father/john_paul_ii/audiences/1999/documents/hf_jp-ii_aud_04081999_en.html. Note also Rev 21:27: "But nothing unclean will enter it, nor anyone who practices abomination or falsehood, but only those who are written in the Lamb's book of life."

37. Ombres, *The Theology of Purgatory*, 73.

38. Thomas J. Bigham, "Redemption through Punishment," *Journal of Pastoral Care* 12 (Fall 1958): 150.

39. Ibid., 155.

40. Ibid.

41. Ibid.

42. John R. Sachs, "Resurrection or Reincarnation? The Christian Doctrine of Purgatory," in *Reincarnation or Resurrection* (Maryknoll, NY: Orbis, 1993), 83. See also Ratzinger, *Eschatology*, 187–89.

43. Josef Pieper, *Faith, Hope, Love* (San Francisco: Ignatius Press, 1997), 281.

44. "Come l'oro, il quale quanto più si fonde, più diventa puro, e quanto più lo fondi, più annuli in lui imperfezione; allo stesso modo agisce il fuoco in tutte le cose materiali, l'anima però non si può annichilire in Dio, ma si annulla in se stessa e quanto più si purifica tanto più si annulla in sé, ma in Dio resta purificata. L'oro, quando è purificato fino a ventiquattro carati, non consuma più per il fuoco che a lui si può

avvincinare, perché il fuoco non può consumare altro, se non la sua imperfezione. Così agisce il fuoco divino con l'anima… dopo aver condotto l'anima alla purificazione, fino a venti-quattro carati, la rende immutabile, perché non le resta più nulla da consumare. Così purificata, anche se fosse tenuta nel fuoco, non sentirebbe alcun dolore; anzi, rimarebbe nel fuoco del Divino Amore per la vita eterna, senza alcuna contrari-età." Caterina da Genova, *Trattato del Purgatorio* (Palermo: Sellerio editore, 2004), 42–43.

45. Arendzen, *Purgatory and Heaven*, 27.

46. Sachs, "Resurrection or Reincarnation?" 83; cf. *Catechism of the Catholic Church* 1472, which, referencing Trent, states that punishment "must not be conceived of as a kind of vengeance inflicted by God from without, but as following from the very nature of sin."

47. Reinhold, "All That Rest in Christ," 301.

48. Sachs, "Resurrection or Reincarnation?" 83.

49. Brown, "No Heaven without Purgatory," 454–55.

50. C. S. Lewis, *Prayer: Letters to Malcolm* (London: Fontana Books, 1974), 111.

51. Bigham, "Redemption through Punishment," 156.

52. Catherine of Genoa, *Catherine of Genoa: Purgation and Purgatory, The Spiritual Dialogues* (Toronto: Paulist Press, 1979), 72.

53. Robert Ombres, "Images of Healing: The Making of the Traditions Concerning Purgatory," *Eastern Churches Review* 8, no. 2 (1976): 131.

54. Aquinas cited in Ombres, "The Doctrine of Purgatory," 284 (IV Sent., dist. XLV, q2 a1 qu2).

55. Arendzen, *Purgatory and Heaven*, 36–37.

56. Ibid., 37.

57. Ibid., 36.

# Chapter 2

1. Zachary Hayes, "The Birth of Purgatory," *Theology Today* 42 (October 1985): 378.

2. See Aaron Milavec, "The Saving Efficacy of the Burning Process in Didache 16.5," in *Didache in Context* (Leiden: E. J. Brill, 1995), 131–55.

3. When asked if any of the fathers taught the doctrine of purgatory, "Respondit Lutherus Ambrosium et Augustinum neque Hieronymum quidem de purgatorio sentire, sed Gregorium visionibus deceptum aliquid docuisse de purgatorio, cum tamen Deus prohiberet nihil esse a Spiritibus explorandum, sed a Mose et prophetis; ideo in hac parte nihil esse Divo Gregorio tribuendum." Milton Gatch, "The Fourth Dialogue of Gregory the Great: Some Problems of Interpretation," *Studia Patristica* 10 (1970).

4. Emmanuel Lanne, "The Teaching of the Catholic Church on Purgatory," *One in Christ* 28, no. 1 (1992): 21.

5. Ibid., 19.

6. There is a common, and mistaken, interpretation of the relationship of Scripture and Tradition in many Catholic circles. This interpretation suggests that Tradition is simply the oral teaching that Jesus gave to the apostles (usually after the resurrection) and that was not recorded in Scripture. In this view, Jesus would have expounded the doctrine of purgatory to his followers, who passed it on to subsequent generations via the unbroken chain of apostolic succession. This view, apart from misunderstanding Catholic teaching regarding the nature of Tradition and of apostolic succession, has no historical or theological grounding. Nevertheless it often is found alongside, and seems to support, suggestions

that an articulate doctrine of purgatory existed in the communities that produced the New Testament.

7. Graham Keith, "Patristic Views on Hell—Part 2," *Evangelical Quarterly* 71, no. 4 (1999): 297.

8. Lanne, "The Teaching of the Catholic Church on Purgatory," 21.

9. For an impressive list of patristic statements in this regard, see James Jorgenson, "The Debate over the Patristic Texts on Purgatory at the Council of Ferrara-Florence, 1438," *St. Vladimir's Theological Quarterly* 30, no. 4 (1986): 313–25.

10. Graham Keith, "Patristic Views on Hell—Part 1," *Evangelical Quarterly* 71, no. 3 (1999): 220.

11. Milavec, "Saving Efficacy," 131.

12. Aaron Milavec, "The Birth of Purgatory: Evidence of the Didache," in *Proceedings, Eastern Great Lakes and Midwest Biblical Societies*, vol. 12 (Cincinnati: Eastern Great Lakes and Midwest Biblical Societies, 1992), 93.

13. Milavec, "Saving Efficacy," 135–36.

14. Lanne, "The Teaching of the Catholic Church on Purgatory," 23.

15. Le Goff, *The Birth of Purgatory*, 53–55. Milavec has noted the same dynamic in *Didache* 5; see Milavec, "Saving Efficacy," 133.

16. Robert B. Eno, "Some Patristic Views on the Relationship of Faith and Works in Justification," *Recherches Augustiniennes* 19 (1984): 25.

17. See Milavec, "Saving Efficacy," 145–51, for an in-depth analysis of fire as the image of God's purifying presence in the Jewish tradition and early Christianity.

18. Ombres, *The Theology of Purgatory*, 36–37.

19. Sixteen hundred years later, C. S. Lewis wrote in the

same vein that "The treatment given will be the one required, whether it hurts little or much." Lewis, *Prayer: Letters to Malcolm*, 111.

20. And indeed, one has been. See Konde Ntedika, *L'évolution de la doctrine du purgatoire chez Saint Augustin* (Paris: Études Augustiniennes, 1966).

21. Graham Keith writes uncomfortably that "Augustine did not altogether rule out the notion of prayer for the dead," and that he did "concede the possibility of post mortem cleansing and forgiveness." Keith, "Patristic Views on Hell—Part 2," 297. Writers more open to such notions do not present Augustine as "not altogether ruling out" or "conceding."

22. Edwards, "Purgatory: 'Birth' or Evolution," 639. Le Goff sees in Augustine four categories (Edwards, "Purgatory: 'Birth' or Evolution," 641): *valde boni, non valde boni, non valde mali,* and *mali.* This schema confuses the issue. The two intermediate terms are not categories in themselves but rather the upper and lower limits of the third category ("blessed but unprepared"). The theology of purgatory presumes, of course, that the third category will eventually collapse into the second ("blessed") and in the end human persons can only end up blessed or condemned.

23. Edwards, "Purgatory: 'Birth' or Evolution," 641.

24. Keith, "Patristic Views on Hell—Part 2," 298.

25. Edwards, "Purgatory: 'Birth' or Evolution," 644.

26. See note 3 above in this chapter.

27. Robert R. Atwell, "From Augustine to Gregory the Great: An Evaluation of the Emergence of the Doctrine of Purgatory," *Journal of Ecclesiastical History* 38, no. 2 (April 1987): 185.

28. Peter McEniery, "Pseudo-Gregory and Purgatory," *Pacifica* 1 (October 1988): 329.

29. Ibid.

30. Francis Clark, *The Pseudo-Gregorian Dialogues* (Leiden: E. J. Brill, 1987).

31. McEniery, "Pseudo-Gregory and Purgatory," 331.

32. Gatch, "The Fourth Dialogue of Gregory the Great," 82.

33. McEniery, "Pseudo-Gregory and Purgatory," 330.

34. Council of Trent, "Decree Concerning Purgatory," in *The Twenty-Fifth Session: Decree Concerning Purgatory*, http://history.hanover.edu/texts/trent/ct25.html.

35. McEniery, "Pseudo-Gregory and Purgatory," 330–31.

36. Ibid., 332.

37. Brian Patrick McGuire, "Purgatory, the Communion of Saints and Medieval Change," *Viator* 20 (1989): 74.

38. Ombres, *The Theology of Purgatory*, 27.

39. Ibid., 41.

40. Ombres, "The Doctrine of Purgatory," 282.

41. Aquinas cited in Ombres, "The Doctrine of Purgatory," 282 (IV Sent., dist XXI, qu1 a1 qu3).

42. It is of interest that Thomas Aquinas died on his way to the Council of Lyons and was not able to participate in the debates held there regarding the doctrine of purgatory. It is hard to imagine a better candidate to represent the Western position.

43. Robert Ombres, "Latins and Greeks in Debate over Purgatory, 1230–1439," *Journal of Ecclesiastical History* 35, no. 1 (January 1984): 11.

44. Ombres, *The Theology of Purgatory*, 45.

45. "Item, si vere penitentes in Dei caritate decesserint, antequam dignis penitentie fructibus de commissis satisfecerint et omissis, eorum animas penis purgatoriis post mortem purgari, et, ut a penis huius modi releventur, prodesse eis fidelium vivorum suffragia, missarum scilicet sacrificia,

orationes et elemosinas et alia pietatis officia, que a fidelibus pro aliis fidelibus fieri consueverunt, secundum ecclesie instituta." *Decrees of the Ecumenical Councils, Volume One: Nicaea I to Lateran V*, ed. Norman P. Tanner, SJ (Sheed & Ward and Georgetown University Press, 1990), 527.

46. See pages 26–27.

47. Ombres, *The Theology of Purgatory*, 47.

48. Ibid., 43.

49. Taylor, "God of Judgment, God of Love," 255.

50. Ibid.

51. Ombres claims that, when studying purgatory, "[i]t soon becomes evident that Purgatory is a test case for revealing much larger concatenations of beliefs, practices, ideologies. With only some exaggeration, it could be said that to ask a Christian what he understands by Purgatory is the quickest way to discover what he believes concerning eschatology and life after death, the relationship of Scripture to Tradition, the nature of the Church, sin and its forgiveness, prayer." Ombres, *The Theology of Purgatory*, 11.

52. For an interesting, though not ecumenically sensitive, discussion of how the rejection of purgatory impacts on theories of atonement, see Hugo A. Meynell, *The Theology of Bernard Lonergan*, American Academy of Religion (Atlanta, GA: Scholars Press, 1986), 119–33.

53. Council of Trent, "Decree Concerning Purgatory."

54. It is important to note that, for ecumenical purposes, nothing more than this bare minimum should stand between dialogue partners. If this issue can be resolved, the doctrine should pose no further impediment to unity.

55. Ombres, *The Theology of Purgatory*, 49.

56. McGuire, "Purgatory, the Communion of Saints and Medieval Change," 83–84.

57. Reinhold, "All That Rest in Christ," 301.

58. Ombres, *The Theology of Purgatory*, 49.

59. Avery Dulles, "John Paul II and the Mystery of the Human Person," *America* 190, no. 3 (February 2, 2004): 21.

60. Ratzinger, *Eschatology*, 228–33.

# Chapter 3

1. Ombres, *The Theology of Purgatory*, 15.

2. There are minorities within Evangelicalism that support the options of Universalism or Annihilationism. These cannot be treated here except to note that they are rejected by the mainstream and that the author hopes that a clear understanding of the insights of purgatory/last judgment might dull the theological impetus for such deviations. There are, of course, Catholics who do not profess the official teaching of their church in this area as much as in any other.

3. Rolheiser, *Purgatory Leads the Dead Soul to Heaven*.

4. Zachary Hayes uses the following formulation: "God is the Last Thing of the creature. Gained, He is its paradise; lost, He is its hell; as demanding, He is its judgment; as cleansing, he is its purgatory." Zachary Hayes, *Visions of a Future: A Study of Christian Eschatology*, New Theology (Wilmington, DE: Michael Glazier, 1989), 113. I have not been able to trace the origin of this saying to my own satisfaction. Hayes claims that it is von Balthasar paraphrasing Augustine and cites Hans Urs von Balthasar, "Eschatology," in *Theology Today*, vol. 2, Johannes Feiner et al. (Milwaukee: The Bruce Publishing Company, 1964), 222–44. On page 228 of this work a similar quote is found, but it is difficult to tell if von Balthasar attributes it to Augustine or is simply

elaborating on the Augustinian phrase "Ipse deus post hanc vitam sic locus noster." In either case, von Balthasar gives no indication as to where either of these is to be found in the Augustinian corpus. Finally, it is unlikely Augustine would have used the noun form for purgatory given that this form is unknown to us until the twelfth century. Regardless, the phrase carries a valuable truth and places the doctrine of purgatory precisely in context.

5. Ombres, *The Theology of Purgatory*, 18.

6. Ibid., 16–17.

7. I am hard pressed between the two: my desire is to depart and be with Christ, for that is far better.

8. Then we who are alive, who are left, will be caught up in the clouds together with them to meet the Lord in the air; and so we will be with the Lord forever.

9. Zachary Hayes, "Hell," in *The New Dictionary of Theology*, ed. Joseph Komonchak, Mary Collins, and Dermot Lane (Collegeville, MN: Michael Glazier, 1987), 459.

10. S. H. T., "Eschatology," in *Evangelical Dictionary of Theology*, ed. J. I. Packer, Sinclair B. Ferguson, and David F. Wright (Downer's Grove, IL: InterVarsity Press, 1988), 231.

11. Timothy R. Phillips, "Hell," in *Evangelical Dictionary of Biblical Theology*, ed. Walter A. Elwell (Grand Rapids, MI: Baker Books, 1996), 339.

12. See Phillips, "Hell," 339, where the author is able to claim on the same page both that "[b]y extrinsically imposing penal conditions on the sinner, God rectifies wrongs and reestablishes his righteous rule" and that "the doors of hell can be locked from the inside."

13. Sachs, "Resurrection or Reincarnation?" 83.

14. Zachary Hayes, "Heaven," in *The New Dictionary of Theology*, ed. Joseph Komonchak, Mary Collins, and Dermot

Lane (Collegeville, MN: Michael Glazier, 1987), 456.

15. Bradford A. Mullen, "Heaven, Heavens, Heavenlies," in *Evangelical Dictionary of Biblical Theology*, ed. Walter A. Elwell (Grand Rapids, MI: Baker Books, 1996), 334.

16. For now we see in a mirror, dimly, but then we will see face to face. Now I know only in part; then I will know fully, even as I have been fully known.

17. F. Q. Gouvea, "Communion of Saints," in *Evangelical Dictionary of Theology, Second Edition*, ed. Walter A. Elwell, (Grand Rapids, MI: Baker Academic, 2001), 277. See also, G. L. B., "Communion of Saints," in *New Dictionary of Theology*, ed. J. I. Packer, Sinclair B. Ferguson, and David F. Wright (Downer's Grove, IL: InterVarsity Press, 1988), 154; Kenan B. Osborne, "Communion of Saints," in *The New Dictionary of Theology*, ed. Joseph Komonchak, Mary Collins, and Dermot Lane (Collegeville, MN: Michael Glazier, 1987), 214–15.

18. Gouvea, "Communion of Saints," 277; G. L. B., "Communion of Saints," 153.

19. Is it possible that postmortem baptisms in the early church were performed for catechumens who died before completing their lengthy catechesis and formal entry into the church, but who were nonetheless considered members of the Body of Christ?

20. Ratzinger, *Eschatology*, 227.

21. Ombres, *The Theology of Purgatory*, 22.

22. Dollard, "Eschatology," 374.

23. It is important to note that he believes Catholicism to teach that human persons can be saved through their own sufferings and that purgatory is a place where those "between the saved and the unsaved" go at death. The Catholic Church does *not* teach such things. John Campbell, "Forgiveness in the Age to Come," *Affirmation & Critique* 9, no. (2004): 61.

24. Campbell, "Forgiveness in the Age to Come," 56.

25. Ibid., 59.

26. Ibid.

27. Ibid., 62.

28. Ibid., 59.

29. It is important to note that it is an unfortunate quirk of language that the same word, prayer, is used to describe addresses to God and intercourse with those alive in Christ with whom we are in communion. Evangelicals are right to insist that God alone is the object of what we might call "prayer proper." Prayer *to* the saints uses the word in the Elizabethan sense of a polite form of address meaning "to ask." Any such prayer generally consists of asking a saint to pray on one's behalf in the same way one would ask one's (biologically living) Christian friends to pray on one's behalf. It is, of course, undeniable that this quirk of language is responsible for much confusion within the Catholic communion about the actual role of the saints, and that many abuses can be traced to it.

30. Ratzinger, *Eschatology*, 233.

31. Avery Dulles, "America's Catholics: What They Believe," *Christianity Today* 30, no. 16 (1986): 25.

32. D.W.A., "Suffering," in *New Dictionary of Theology*, ed. J. I. Packer, Sinclair B. Ferguson, and David F. Wright (Downer's Grove, IL: InterVarsity Press, 1988), 668.

33. J. S. Feinberg, "Pain," in *Evangelical Dictionary of Theology, Second Edition*, ed. Walter A. Elwell (Grand Rapids, MI: Baker Academic, 2001), 883.

34. Ibid., 882.

35. D. W. A., "Suffering," 668.

36. Barry D. Smith, "Suffering," in *Evangelical Dictionary of Biblical Theology*, ed. Walter A. Elwell (Grand Rapids, MI: Baker Books, 1996), 752.

37. Dulles, "John Paul II and the Mystery of the Human Person," 21.

38. Ombres, *The Theology of Purgatory*, 24.

39. Bryan E. Beyer, "Presence of God," in *Evangelical Dictionary of Biblical Theology*, ed. Walter A. Elwell (Grand Rapids, MI: Baker Books, 1996), 630.

40. They heard the sound of the Lord God walking in the garden at the time of the evening breeze, and the man and his wife hid themselves from the presence of the Lord God among the trees of the garden.

41. But nothing unclean will enter it, nor anyone who practices abomination or falsehood, but only those who are written in the Lamb's book of life.

42. Beyer, "Presence of God," 630.

43. G. W. Bromiley, "Presence, Divine," in *Evangelical Dictionary of Theology, Second Edition*, ed. Walter A. Elwell (Grand Rapids, MI: Baker Academic, 2001), 952.

44. This reality reinforces our understanding of why we needed a mediator both God and human.

45. For a useful summary, see R. L. Shelton, "Perfection, Perfectionism," in *Evangelical Dictionary of Theology, Second Edition*, ed. Walter A. Elwell (Grand Rapids, MI: Baker Academic, 2001), 903–6.

46. Robert W. Yarbrough, "Perfect, Perfection," in *Evangelical Dictionary of Biblical Theology*, ed. Walter A. Elwell (Grand Rapids, MI: Baker Books, 1996), 599.

# Chapter 4

1. I speak here with experience of North American Evangelicals only and suspect, for reasons elaborated below,

that these generalizations would not necessarily apply to the global Evangelical community.

2. See, for example, Miroslav Volf, *Exclusion and Embrace: A Theological Exploration of Identity, Otherness, and Reconciliation* (Nashville: Abingdon Press, 1996), 301–4.

3. Volf, *Exclusion and Embrace*, 138.

4. Perhaps the most dangerous possibility here is simply to assume that God is on one's side and that one's enemies will be condemned to hell. There are at least two problems here. The first is that, even if your enemy is in hell, heaven will not be heaven for you if you are unable to forgive, so at some point *you* must stop pursuing conflict. The second is a matter of simple logic: if God is on one side or the other, you have, at best, only a 50 percent chance of being vindicated in the end. Counting on the damnation of the enemy will not do.

5. Volf, "Reconciled in the End."

6. Miroslav Volf, "Love Your Heavenly Enemy," *Christianity Today* 44 (October 2000): 94.

7. Volf, "The Final Reconciliation," 91–92.

8. Volf, "The Final Reconciliation," 92; Volf, "Love Your Heavenly Enemy," 95; Volf, "Reconciled in the End."

9. I use the term "formulations" rather than "theology" here to indicate that Catholic *theology* affirms only a painful postmortem process of purification in which the faithful may be aided by prayer. There is no reason that this cannot be understood as part of the broader event of the judgment. In any case, it is perilous to set out timelines of the afterlife with a degree of certainty that could be considered so binding as to be a barrier to communion. Human thought and language struggle so much in discussing such things that to insist on a particular imaginative conception of the afterlife as essential to authentic Christian faith is

simply foolish. The Congregation for the Doctrine of the Faith teaches that, "[w]hen dealing with man's situation after death, one must especially be aware of arbitrary imaginative representations; excess of this kind is a major cause of the difficulties that Christian faith often encounters [in the realm of eschatology]. Respect must, however, be given to the images employed in the Scriptures. Their profound meaning must be discerned, while avoiding the risk of over-attenuating them, since this often empties of substance the realities designated by the images." Congregation for the Doctrine of the Faith, "Letter on Certain Questions Concerning Eschatology" (1979), Http://www.catholicculture.org/library/view.cfm?recnum = 4382.

10. Hayes, *Visions of a Future*, 113. See note 4, chapter 3.

11. Ntedika, *L'évolution de la doctrine du purgatoire*, 67–68. See also McEniery, "Pseudo-Gregory and Purgatory," 329–30.

12. Milavec, "Saving Efficacy," 145–51.

13. The difference between the judgment entries in the first and second editions of the *Evangelical Dictionary of Theology* provides a striking example of this paradox. The first entry insists that "there will be a final judgment...and all face it (Heb 12:23)." Leon Morris, "Judgment," in *Evangelical Dictionary of Biblical Theology*, ed. Walter A. Elwell (Grand Rapids, MI: Baker Books, 1996), 437. Five years later, in the second edition, another author suggests John's Gospel teaches that "believers do not go through judgment but have already crossed from death to life (5:24)." D. A. Hubbard, "Last Judgment," in *Evangelical Dictionary of Theology, Second Edition*, ed. Walter A. Elwell (Grand Rapids, MI: Baker Academic, 2001), 671. It should be noted that many translations render the verb in question in the passage from John's

Gospel to read "condemned." That is, believers will be judged, but will not be condemned.

14. A. Willingale, "The Last Judgment: In Protestant Theology from Orthodoxy to Ritschl," *Evangelical Quarterly* 36 (1964): 110.

15. Leon Morris writes, for instance, that because our judge is our savior, we can be assured "that the final judgment will be a judgment of love. But it does not mean that judgment ceases to be a grim reality. The self-sacrificing love we see on Calvary is in itself the most damning judgment imaginable on the self-seeking life." Leon Morris, *The Biblical Doctrine of Judgment* (London: The Tyndale Press, 1960), 61–62. Morris's work is, on the whole, quite commendable. He fails, however, to make any hypothesis as to what such a "damning judgment" might mean for those who are not, in fact, damned.

16. "It is a fearful thing to fall into the hands of the living God."

17. Stephen H. Travis, "The Problem of Judgment," *Themelios* 11, no. 2 (1986): 53; S. H. T., "Judgment of God," in *New Dictionary of Theology*, ed. J. I. Packer, Sinclair B. Ferguson, and David F. Wright (Downer's Grove, IL: InterVarsity Press, 1988), 358; Morris, *The Biblical Doctrine of Judgment*, 66.

18. See, for example, Mark A. Seifrid, "Justified by Faith and Judged by Works: A Biblical Paradox and Its Significance," *Southern Baptist Journal of Theology* 5, no. 4 (2001): 84–97; S. H. T., "Judgment of God," 358; Daniel Lamont, "Tests in the Final Judgment," *Evangelical Quarterly* 7, no. 4 (1935): 351; Morris, *The Biblical Doctrine of Judgment*, 67. Morris, interestingly, appeals to 1 Cor 3:10–15 to resolve the problem, the same Scripture passage that has been most

important in the development of the Catholic teaching on purgatory.

19. Volf, "Enter into Joy!" 263.

20. In a different context Volf writes: "Imagine this: God pronounces judgment and you say, 'This is outrageous! You blew my offense totally out of proportion and you forgot a number of my opponent's transgressions. I will get myself a new lawyer and appeal.'" Volf, "Love Your Heavenly Enemy," 97.

21. Seifrid, "Justified by Faith," 91.

22. Volf, "Love Your Heavenly Enemy," 97 He notes here that those in heaven "have been given their true identity by being freed from sin."

23. See Volf, *Exclusion and Embrace*, 138 (and following) for Volf's thought concerning the grace of forgetting.

24. Volf, "Enter into Joy!" 262, 277.

25. Volf, *Exclusion and Embrace*, 294.

26. Volf, "The Final Reconciliation."

27. Miroslav Volf, "Memory of Reconciliation—Reconciliation of Memory," opening address in *Proceedings of the Fifty-Ninth Annual Convention*, vol. 59, ed. Richard C. Sparks (Weston, VA: The Catholic Theological Society of America, 2003), 11.

28. See Morris, *The Biblical Doctrine of Judgment*, 63–64; Gabriel J. Fackre, "Eschatology and Systematics," *Ex Auditu* 6 (1990): 105; Eberhard Jüngel, "The Last Judgment as an Act of Grace," *Louvain Studies* 15 (1990): 397.

29. Volf, "Love Your Heavenly Enemy," 97.

30. Ibid., 96.

31. Volf, *Exclusion and Embrace*, 111–19.

32. In N. T. Wright, *Evil and the Justice of God* (Downer's Grove, IL: InterVarsity Press, 2006), 158–59, Wright wisely notes that, in his parable in Matt 18 about the servant who

was forgiven his debts by the king, but would not release his fellow servant from a much smaller debt, Jesus "is telling us, in effect, that the faculty we have for receiving forgiveness and the faculty we have for granting forgiveness are one and the same thing." The person who insists on strict justice from his neighbor is the one who does not recognize the weight of the claims of justice on himself.

33. Volf, "The Final Reconciliation," 98–99.

34. Ibid., 102.

35. Volf, "Enter into Joy!" 257.

36. Ibid., 276–77.

37. Volf, *Exclusion and Embrace*, 297.

38. See pages 7–8.

39. Volf, "Enter into Joy!" 261.

40. Ibid.

41. Volf, "Enter into Joy!" 261 See note 26 in Volf.

42. Volf, "The Final Reconciliation," 93.

43. The Catholic-Lutheran Joint Declaration on Justification indicates that differences on this issue were more a matter of theological emphasis than of mutually exclusive doctrines and, as such, Catholics could affirm something as authentic to Christianity while recognizing that the language used is not employed in the way that the Catholic tradition has typically employed it. Lutheran World Federation and the Catholic Church, *Joint Declaration on the Doctrine of Justification* (1999) http://www.vatican.va/roman_curia/ pontifical_councils/chrstuni/documents/rc_pc_chrstuni_doc _31101999_cath-luth-joint-declaration_en.html.

44. Karl P. Donfried, "Justification and Last Judgment in Paul," *Interpretation* 30 (1976): 143.

45. The reader may note here a small problem: have I not, by accepting Volf's conclusions about the judgment and

paralleling them with purgatory, abandoned the Catholic position that not everyone requires purgatory? According to Volf it would be impossible for anyone's full justification (or sanctification) to take place outside the context of the final judgment. Certainly, it would be useful here to have access to Professor Etzelmüller's thought. Nevertheless, the problem is possible to overcome without much difficulty. Those whom the Catholic tradition understands as having been so perfected in this life as to have no need of purgatory would undergo the same process as everyone else at the judgment with one difference: their abandonment of self and reliance on Christ would already be so complete that what is intensely painful for others would be to them only joy. If all Christians were so disposed at the judgment, Catholics would seem even to endorse the common Evangelical position critiqued at the beginning of this chapter, i.e., that the judgment for those in Christ will not be severe. If, however, *all* those in Christ were *always* seen to be *fully* abandoned of self and *completely* reliant upon him, there would have been no impetus for either the doctrine of purgatory, Professor Volf's theology of reconciliation, or this book.

46. Ratzinger, *Eschatology*, 230.

47. Volf, "The Final Reconciliation," 99.

48. Ibid., 97.

49. Volf, *Exclusion and Embrace*, 120.

50. Ibid., 125.

51. This is quoted from memory and may not be entirely accurate. It is hoped that the point is well taken, regardless.

52. Volf, *Exclusion and Embrace*, 138.

53. The reader will recall David Brown's argument, recounted on pages 16–17 herein, that subjects of such a process would have little reason for identifying themselves

with the perfected persons into whom they seem to have been changed.

54. Volf, "The Final Reconciliation," 103.

55. Volf, "Enter into Joy!" 264.

56. Quoted in Volf, "The Final Reconciliation," 107.

57. Volf, "The Final Reconciliation," 99.

58. So when you are offering your gift at the altar, if you remember that your brother or sister has something against you, leave your gift there before the altar and go; first be reconciled to your brother or sister, and then come and offer your gift.

59. Volf, "The Final Reconciliation," 101.

60. Ibid., 93.

61. Fackre, "Eschatology and Systematics," 109.

62. Volf, "Love Your Heavenly Enemy," 95.

63. Volf, "Enter into Joy!" 259.

64. Karl Rahner, "Purgatory," in *Faith and Ministry*, vol. XIX, Theological Investigations (New York: Crossroad, 1983), 191; Michael Stoeber, *Reclaiming Theodicy: Reflections on Suffering, Compassion and Spiritual Transformation* (Hampshire: Palgrave Macmillan, 2005), 94–97.

65. I am accusing neither Rahner nor Stoeber of endorsing such extreme positions, but merely note the caution necessary when engaging these ideas.

66. Volf, *Exclusion and Embrace*. Again, pages 111–19 offer an important synthesis , but to capture the broad sweep of Volf's thought, reading the entire text cannot be too highly recommended.

# Conclusion

1. See Joe Mizzi, "Catholics and Evangelicals Divided," http://www.justforcatholics.org/ecumenism.htm. In the article Dr. Mizzi, the head of Just For Catholics, writes: "Each one of us must take his stand. You are either an evangelical, earnestly contending for the faith that was delivered to the saints, or an ecumenist, sacrificing Truth on the altar of a false unity. You must choose. Do you love Catholics enough to warn them of their peril and to proclaim to them the Gospel for their salvation? Or would you rather mock them, calling them 'brothers and sisters in Christ' while you escort them on their way to hell?"

2. Joe Mizzi, "Purgatory or Christ," http://www.justfor catholics.org/a93.htm.

3. Ibid.

4. In his second encyclical, *Spe Salvi*, released after the completion of this manuscript, Benedict XVI includes a reflection on the doctrine of purgatory in his third section, "Judgement as a setting for learning and practicing hope." It can be nerve-wracking to have the pope write a reflection on one's topic immediately after one has completed one's work, but I am happy to report that Benedict's insights seem to me entirely compatible with the thrust of this work (or perhaps more important, the thrust of this work seems entirely compatible with the insights of Benedict XVI). In any case, I highly recommend his recent, and earlier, work to the reader.

5. Ratzinger, *Eschatology*, 229.

6. Jüngel, "The Last Judgment," 397–98. Recall Volf, "The Final Reconciliation," 98–99. There Volf argued that judgment/reconciliation was facilitated precisely by the

Christ who had both suffered in solidarity with victims and for sins of the perpetrators.

7. Jüngel, "The Last Judgment," 396.

8. Ibid., 401.

9. See pages 35–37.

10. Furthermore, it is hoped that the proposal I have made for understanding our actions vis-à-vis the dead in purgatory as acts of love which, by the very nature of love, bring those to whom they are directed closer to love itself, will make such practices more coherent to Evangelical Christianity. See pages 29–31.

11. It is not necessary for unity that Evangelicals take up the practice of prayer for the dead, but it is necessary that they refrain from condemning the idea as *ipso facto* contrary to authentic Christianity. The possibility for Evangelicals to critique particular Catholic practices that may venture into the realm of the magical, mechanical, or superstitious should not only be left open, but should be regarded as one of the blessings of ecumenical dialogue.

12. Ratzinger, *Eschatology*, 227.

13. In Anthony Kelly, *Eschatology and Hope*, Theology in Global Perspective (Maryknoll, NY: Orbis Books, 2006), 123–32, Kelly gives a sensitive and lucid treatment of purgatory that does address these issues. On page 124, he sees purgatory as one way of talking about the particular judgment, while on page 128 he suggests that such a purgatory leads to the universal judgment understood, with Volf, whom he cites, as the universal reconciliation.

14. S. H. T., "Eschatology," in *New Dictionary of Theology*, ed. J. I. Packer, Sinclair B. Ferguson, and David F. Wright (Downer's Grove, IL: InterVarsity Press, 1988), 230.

# BIBLIOGRAPHY

## Books

Arendzen, J. P. *Purgatory and Heaven*. New York: Sheed and Ward, 1960.

Augustine of Hippo. "On the Trinity: Book Eight, Chapter 17." In *Augustine of Hippo: Selected Writings*, ed. Mary T. Clark. New York: Paulist Press, 1984, 356–57.

Bartmann, Bernhard. *Purgatory: A Book of Christian Comfort*. London: Burns Oates & Washbourne, Ltd, 1936.

Caterina da Genova. *Trattato del Purgatorio*. Palermo: Sellerio editore, 2004.

Catherine of Genoa. *Catherine of Genoa: Purgation and Purgatory—the Spiritual Dialogues*. Toronto: Paulist Press, 1979.

Clark, Francis. *The Pseudo-Gregorian Dialogues*. Leiden: E. J. Brill, 1987.

Hayes, Zachary. *Visions of a Future: A Study of Christian Eschatology. New Theology Studies* 8. Wilmington, DE: Michael Glazier, 1989.

Kelly, Anthony. *Eschatology and Hope*. Theology in Global Perspective. Maryknoll, NY: Orbis Books, 2006.

Le Goff, Jacques. *The Birth of Purgatory*. Chicago: University of Chicago Press, 1984.

Lewis, C. S. *Prayer: Letters to Malcolm*. London: Fontana Books, 1974.

Meynell, Hugo A. *The Theology of Bernard Lonergan*. American Academy of Religion. Atlanta, GA: Scholars Press, 1986.

Morris, Leon. *The Biblical Doctrine of Judgment*. London: The Tyndale Press, 1960.

Mother Mary of St. Austin. *The Divine Crucible of Purgatory*. New York: P. J. Kenedy & Sons, 1940.

Ntedika, Konde. *L'évolution de la doctrine du purgatoire chez Saint Augustin*. Paris: Études Augustiniennes, 1966.

Ombres, Robert. *The Theology of Purgatory*. Dublin: Mercier Press, 1980.

Pieper, Josef. *Faith, Hope, Love*. San Francisco: Ignatius Press, 1997.

Ratzinger, Joseph. *Eschatology: Death and Eternal Life*. Dogmatic Theology. Washington DC: The Catholic University of America Press, 1988.

Sayers, Dorothy L. "Introduction to The *Comedy* of Dante Alighieri the Florentine." In *The* Comedy *of Dante Alighieri the Florentine, Cantica II: Purgatory*, 9–72. Harmondsworth: Penguin Books, 1981.

Shouppe, F. X. *Purgatory: Illustrated by the Lives and Legends of the Saints*. Rockford, IL: Tan Books and Publishers, Inc., 1973.

Stoeber, Michael. *Reclaiming Theodicy: Reflections on Suffering, Compassion and Spiritual Transformation*. Hampshire: Palgrave Macmillan, 2005.

Volf, Miroslav. *Exclusion and Embrace: A Theological Exploration of Identity, Otherness, and Reconciliation*. Nashville: Abingdon Press, 1996.

Wright, N. T. *Evil and the Justice of God*. Downer's Grove, IL: InterVarsity Press, 2006.

# Articles

Anglican-Orthodox Dialogue. "The Communion of Saints and the Departed." *Sobornost* 3 (1981): 93–96.

Atwell, Robert R. "From Augustine to Gregory the Great: An Evaluation of the Emergence of the Doctrine of Purgatory." *Journal of Ecclesiastical History* 38, no. 2 (April 1987): 173–86.

Betty, L. Stafford. "The Great Chain of Being in the Lives of the Faithful: The Status of Purgatory Today." In *Fragments of Infinity*. Dorset, UK: Prism, 1991, 21–30.

Beyer, Bryan E. "Presence of God." In *Evangelical Dictionary of Biblical Theology*, ed. Walter A. Elwell. Grand Rapids, MI: Baker Books, 1996, 629–30.

Bigham, Thomas J. "Redemption through Punishment." *Journal of Pastoral Care* 12 (Fall 1958): 149–58.

Bromiley, G. W. "Presence, Divine." In *Evangelical Dictionary of Theology, Second Edition*, ed. Walter A. Elwell. Grand Rapids, MI: Baker Academic, 2001, 951–52.

Brown, David. "No Heaven without Purgatory." *Religious Studies* 21, no. 4 (December 1985): 447–56.

Campbell, John. "Forgiveness in the Age to Come." *Affirmation & Critique* 9, no. 1 (2004): 56–69.

Congregation for the Doctrine of the Faith. "Letter on Certain Questions Concerning Eschatology," 1979. Http://www.catholicculture.org/library/view.cfm?recnum=4382.

Council of Trent. "Decree Concerning Purgatory." In *The Twenty-Fifth Session: Decree Concerning Purgatory*. Http://history.hanover.edu/texts/trent/ct25.html.

Dollard, Jerome R. "Eschatology: A Roman Catholic Perspective." *Review and Expositor* 79 (1982): 367–80.

Donfried, Karl P. "Justification and Last Judgment in Paul." *Interpretation* 30 (1976): 140–52.

Dulles, Avery. "America's Catholics: What They Believe." *Christianity Today* 30, no. 16 (1986): 23–27.

————. "John Paul II and the Mystery of the Human Person." *America* 190, no. 3 (February 2, 2004): 10–22.

D. W. A. "Suffering." In *New Dictionary of Theology*. Ed. J. I. Packer, Sinclair B. Ferguson, and David F. Wright. Downer's Grove, IL: InterVarsity Press, 1988, 667–69.

Edwards, Graham. "Purgatory: 'Birth' or Evolution." *Journal of Ecclesiastical History* 36, no. 4 (October 1985): 634–46.

Eno, Robert B. "Some Patristic Views on the Relationship of Faith and Works in Justification." *Recherches Augustiniennes* 19 (1984): 3–27.

Fackre, Gabriel J. "Eschatology and Systematics." *Ex Auditu* 6 (1990): 101–17.

Feinberg, J. S. "Pain." In *Evangelical Dictionary of Theology, Second Edition*, edited by Walter A. Elwell. Grand Rapids, MI: Baker Academic, 2001: 882–83.

G. L. B. "Communion of Saints." In *New Dictionary of Theology*, edited by J. I. Packer, Sinclair B. Ferguson, and David F. Wright. Downer's Grove, IL: InterVarsity Press, 1988, 152–53.

Gatch, Milton. "The Fourth Dialogue of Gregory the Great: Some Problems of Interpretation." *Studia Patristica* 10 (1970): 77–83.

Gouvea, F. Q. "Communion of Saints." In *Evangelical Dictionary of Theology, Second Edition*, edited by Walter A. Elwell. Grand Rapids, MI: Baker Academic, 2001, 277–78.

Hayes, Zachary. "The Birth of Purgatory." *Theology Today* 42 (October 1985): 376–78.

————. "Heaven." In *The New Dictionary of Theology*, edited by Joseph Komonchak, Mary Collins, and Dermot Lane. Collegeville, MN: Michael Glazier, 1987, 454–56.

————. "Hell." In *The New Dictionary of Theology*, edited by Joseph Komonchak, Mary Collins, and Dermot Lane. Collegeville, MN: Michael Glazier, 1987, 457–59.

Horne, Brian L. "Where Is Purgatory?" In *"If Christ Be Not Risen."* San Francisco: Collins Liturgical, 1988, 92–100.

Hubbard, D. A. "Last Judgment." In *Evangelical Dictionary of Theology, Second Edition*, edited by Walter A. Elwell. Grand Rapids, MI: Baker Academic, 2001, 671–72.

John Paul II. "General Audience." In *General Audience, Wednesday 4 August 1999*. Http://www.vatican.va/holy _father/john_paul_ii/audiences/1999/documents/hf_ jp-ii_aud_04081999_en.html.

Jorgenson, James. "The Debate over the Patristic Texts on Purgatory at the Council of Ferrara-Florence, 1438." *St. Vladimir's Theological Quarterly* 30, no. 4 (1986): 309–34.

Jüngel, Eberhard. "The Last Judgment as an Act of Grace." *Louvain Studies* 15 (1990): 389–405.

Keith, Graham. "Patristic Views on Hell—Part 1." *Evangelical Quarterly* 71, no. 3 (1999): 217–32.

————. "Patristic Views on Hell—Part 2." *Evangelical Quarterly* 71, no. 4 (1999): 291–310.

Lamont, Daniel. "Tests in the Final Judgment." *Evangelical Quarterly* 7, no. 4 (1935): 351–63.

Lanne, Emmanuel. "The Teaching of the Catholic Church on Purgatory." *One in Christ* 28, no. 1 (1992): 13–30.

Lutheran World Federation and the Catholic Church. *Joint Declaration on the Doctrine of Justification*, 1999. Http://www.vatican.va/roman_curia/pontifical_councils /chrstuni/documents/rc_pc_chrstuni_doc_31101999_ cath-luth-joint-declaration_en.html.

McEniery, Peter. "Pseudo-Gregory and Purgatory." *Pacifica* 1 (October 1988): 328–34.

McGuire, Brian Patrick. "Purgatory, the Communion of Saints and Medieval Change." *Viator* 20 (1989): 61–84.

Milavec, Aaron. "The Birth of Purgatory: Evidence of the *Didache*." In *Proceedings, Eastern Great Lakes and Midwest Biblical Societies*, vol. 12. Cincinnati: Eastern Great Lakes and Midwest Biblical Societies, 1992, 91–104.

———. "The Saving Efficacy of the Burning Process in *Didache* 16.5." In *Didache in Context*. Leiden: E. J. Brill, 1995, 131–55.

Mizzi, Joe. "Catholics and Evangelicals Divided." Http://www.justforcatholics.org/ecumenism.htm.

———. "Purgatory or Christ." Http://www.justfor catholics.org/a93.htm.

Morris, Leon. "Judgment." In *Evangelical Dictionary of Biblical Theology*, edited by Walter A. Elwell. Grand Rapids, MI: Baker Books, 1996, 436–37.

Mullen, Bradford A. "Heaven, Heavens, Heavenlies." In *Evangelical Dictionary of Biblical Theology*, edited by Walter A. Elwell. Grand Rapids, MI: Baker Books, 1996, 332–35.

Ombres, Robert. "The Doctrine of Purgatory According to St. Thomas Aquinas." *Downside Review* 99 (October 1981): 279–87.

————. "Images of Healing: The Making of the Traditions Concerning Purgatory." *Eastern Churches Review* 8, no. 2 (1976): 128–38.

————. "Latins and Greeks in Debate Over Purgatory, 1230–1439." *Journal of Ecclesiastical History* 35, no. 1 (January 1984): 1–14.

Osborne, Kenan B. "Communion of Saints." In *The New Dictionary of Theology*, edited by Joseph Komonchak, Mary Collins, and Dermot Lane. Collegeville, MN: Michael Glazier, 1987, 213–16.

Phillips, Timothy R. "Hell." In *Evangelical Dictionary of Biblical Theology*, edited by Walter A. Elwell. Grand Rapids, MI: Baker Books, 1963, 38–40.

Rahner, Karl. "Purgatory." In *Faith and Ministry*, vol. XIX. Theological Investigations. New York: Crossroad, 1983.

Reinhold, H. A. "All That Rest in Christ." *Worship* 26, no. 6 (1952): 298–303.

Rolheiser, Ron. *Purgatory Leads the Dead Soul to Heaven*, 2003. Http://www.wcr.ab.ca/columns/rolheiser/2003/rolheiser120103.shtml.

R. T. D. "Purgatory." In *New Dictionary of Theology*, edited by J. I. Packer, Sinclair B. Ferguson, and David. Wright, Downer's Grove, IL: InterVarsity Press, 1988, 549–50.

Sachs, John R. "Resurrection or Reincarnation? The Christian Doctrine of Purgatory." In *Reincarnation or Resurrection*. Maryknoll, NY: Orbis, 1993, 81–87.

Seifrid, Mark A. "Justified by Faith and Judged by Works: A Biblical Paradox and Its Significance." Southern Baptist Journal of Theology 5, no. 4 (2001): 84–97.

Shelton, R. L. "Perfection, Perfectionism." In *Evangelical Dictionary of Theology, Second Edition*, edited by Walter A. Elwell. Grand Rapids, MI: Baker Academic, 2001, 902–6.

S. H. T. "Eschatology." In *New Dictionary of Theology*, edited by J. I. Packer, Sinclair B. Ferguson, and David F. Wright. Downer's Grove, IL: InterVarsity Press, 1988, 228–31.

———. "Judgment of God." In *New Dictionary of Theology*, edited by J. I. Packer, Sinclair B. Ferguson, and David F. Wright. Downer's Grove, IL: InterVarsity Press, 1988, 358.

Smith, Barry D. "Suffering." In *Evangelical Dictionary of Biblical Theology*, edited by Walter A. Elwell. Grand Rapids, MI: Baker Books, 1996, 749–52.

Taylor, Larissa Juliet. "God of Judgment, God of Love: Catholic Preaching in France, 1460–1560." *Historical Reflections* 26, no. 2 (2000): 247–68.

Travis, Stephen H. "The Problem of Judgment." *Themelios* 11, no. 2 (1986): 52–57.

Urs von Balthasar, Hans. "Eschatology." In *Theology Today*, vol. 2, Johannes Feiner et al. Milwaukee: The Bruce Publishing Company, 1964, 222–44.

Volf, Miroslav. "Enter into Joy! Sin, Death, and the Life of the World to Come." In *End of the World and the Ends of God*. Harrisburg, PA: Trinity Press International, 2000, 256–78.

———. "The Final Reconciliation: Reflections on a Social Dimension of the Eschatological Transition." *Modern Theology* 16, no. 1 (January 2000): 91–113.

———. "Love Your Heavenly Enemy." *Christianity Today* 44 (October 2000): 94–97.

————. "Memory of Reconciliation—Reconciliation of Memory." Opening address in *Proceedings of the Fifty-Ninth Annual Convention*, vol. 59, ed. Richard C. Sparks. Weston, VA: The Catholic Theological Society of America, 2003, 1–13.

————. "Reconciled in the End." *Christian Century* 116 (1999): 1098.

Walls, Jerry L. "Purgatory for Everyone." *First Things* 122 (April 2002): 26–30.

White, R. E. O. "Sanctification." In *Evangelical Dictionary of Theology, Second Edition*, edited by Walter A. Elwell. Grand Rapids, MI: Baker Academic, 2001, 1051–54.

Willingale, A. "The Last Judgment: In Protestant Theology from Orthodoxy to Ritschl." *Evangelical Quarterly* 36 (1964): 109–11.

Yarbrough, Robert W. "Perfect, Perfection." In *Evangelical Dictionary of Biblical Theology*, edited by Walter A. Elwell. Grand Rapids, MI: Baker Books, 1996, 598–99.